Old Boston:
As Wild As They Come

City well at the intersection of 9th and Main Street in
Old Boston, Colorado 1887.[1]

Front Cover: The top picture on the cover is called "The Cowboy Funeral" and is the only known picture of the regulator Bill Thompson (center). The bottom picture is the well at the intersection of 9th and Main in Old Boston, Colorado.

Back Cover: Sunset picture was taken by the author in December 2017 on the location which would have been South Main Street in Boston, Colorado 129 years after the demise of the town.

HAPPY 77TH BIRTHDAY
IT's NICE TO MEET SOMEONE
WHO WAS THERE ☺ ALL MY
BEST.
                    Kent Brooks
          7 – 18 – 2018

Old Boston:
As Wild As They Come

Compiled and Annotated

By

Kent Brooks

First Printing: 2018

ISBN 978-1732258501

Lonesome Prairie Publications
PO Box 842
Casper, WY 82601

www.lonesomeprairie.com

Ordering Information:

Special discounts are available on quantity purchases by corporations, associations, educators, and others. For details, contact the publisher at the above listed address

Dedication

To my lovely wife who before this project said, "You should write a book" and who after I started said, "You're gonna' finish."

Thank you. Without your support and patience, I would have never achieved this dream.

Contents

Acknowledgements

I would like to thank my teachers, my angry 'stabby' editors who went after this with their red pens blazing (you know who you are), my classmates over the years from kindergarten to graduate school, and my family and friends who had to listen to these stories over and over and over...without your help this book would never have been completed. Thank you for your patience and guidance. A special thanks to those who documented other parts of Baca County Colorado history in the past,

- JR Austin, *"An Early History of Baca County"* (1936)
- James Hill, *"A History of Baca County"* Thesis (1941)
- Ike Osteen, *"A Place Called Baca"* (1979)
- Iris Caldwell, *"Bear Tracks and Cactus Trees"* (1980)
- Amy Rogers Venter, Baca County History, *"The Thirties"* (1989)

I really can't imagine putting one of these things together with a typewriter and without access to digital archives the way all of those folks did. Thanks Top of the Nation Enterprises for your guidance and assistance with the design of the cover.

Thanks to Val Millican, Baca County Museum Director and the Baca County Commissioners for access to resources at the Baca County Museum whenever I was able to come wandering home. Thanks to the Historical Societies of Kansas, Colorado and Oklahoma, the Texas and Southwest Cattle Raiser's Association and the Denver Public Library. What incredible treasures are held at each of these places.

Thanks to my mother, a Baca County baby, a great teller of Baca County stories, and the person who would have loved this project more than anyone else reading this text. Thank you God in heaven for the ability to work. With my brother, who had cerebral palsy, specifically in mind not everyone is given that gift. I am humbled I got the opportunity to work on compiling the history of Boston, Colorado, although this project never really seemed like work.

Foreword

Taking nothing at face value, Kent Brooks, researches and documents every piece of information that he can find. I know he has spent countless hours during the past 2 years, locating, collecting, verifying and documenting hundreds of pieces of written information in the Baca County Museum. In his quest for information, he has also interviewed many people and researched in Kansas, Oklahoma, New Mexico, and Texas, as well as newspapers across the United States.

It is through this dedication that Kent has been able to piece together the stories of "Old Boston" and the people who settled there.

"Old Boston: Wild As They Come" is unique in that it brings life to characters like Sam Konkel and others. Kent has succeeded in weaving the true events of those days into an entertaining technically accurate and informative book.

I look forward to many more books compiled and written by Kent Brooks.

Val Millican, Director
Baca County Colorado Museum

Introduction

I often heard bits and pieces of the story of Old Boston while growing up on the vast plains of Southeast Colorado. Many of my relatives still live in present-day Baca County, the most Southeast County in the state of Colorado. My cousin farms a piece of ground which was the homestead of Dr. Thomas Milligan, who is part of this story. During my high school and college days I had the opportunity to work for them and drove past the Boston town site many times, not understanding the history of this location. I use the term town site very loosely as nothing exists today which would indicate the town existed. The location is at the intersection of two country roads and with the exception of a few family names, Capansky, Lepel, and Konkel no other decedents of this story remained in the area into the modern age. In local lore, Old Boston was a disorderly and dangerous little boom town. It sprouted on the southeast Colorado prairie in 1886 to catch the railroad heading west to Trinidad, Colorado and to become the county seat of a new Colorado county. Its founders also intended for it to service the commerce needs of homesteaders pouring into the area to acquire free land from the government. The term "Old Boston" is more of a local reference rather than a reference to its age. Established in 1886, it is comparatively much younger than its New England namesake, which people would naturally think of when hearing the name.

Within these pages are tales of people who walked the streets of the old town. Stories of horse thieves, gambling, drinking, shootings, and lynchings, overshadowed the story of the typical settler hoping to file a homestead claim and get their own place. Faced with this "old west law and order" there were attempts to maintain civilization amid disorder. Yes, there was plenty of old west style violence and shootings, but the stories about the lives of everyday and sometimes quirky characters of Boston is what makes this tale unique. Unlike the fictional tales in many western novels and the made up stories of Hollywood's big screen, this place existed, real people lived here, and the events described in these pages happened. Al Jennings, who walked the streets of Old Boston was a consultant and actor in many early silent Western movies and likely influenced the entire genre of western movies. His time in Boston certainly influenced his "old west" worldview.

The primary resource for this narrative is the 1918 and 1919 writing of the editor of one of Old Boston's newspapers, Sam Konkel. I have attempted to retain his original writing as much as possible, as his perspective gives this story much of its flavor. Konkel's writing also corrects minor historical flaws in previous local discussions about Boston. Various terms such as "cow boys" and "billyards" represent the time and place and Konkel's style and charm. Cow boys when separated has in some cases been determined to be a derogatory term. Whether or not Konkel meant it to be derogatory will never really be known. The other spelling variations may simply have occurred when he ran out of a particular letter when setting up the press to run an issue of his paper. An advertisement for the Star Billiard and Saloon spells "Billiard" how we would spell the word "Billiard" while in the Boston write-ups Konkel uses the alternate, "billyard" spelling. Maybe the answer is as simple as he ran out of letters on his printing press. Most variations in spelling remain as they were and I have maintained some headers from the newspaper articles to provide some perspective on how the original material was presented. Slang terms of the day such as "mummixed" and newspaper abbreviations such as "prox." also remain. The term "prox." essentially means next, and is used in old newspapers to indicate the upcoming month.

The core content is documented with endnotes, but I am also using a few footnotes within the text when I need to identify an issue, an error, or just point out information.

Konkel also described the Jennings clan as the "Jenningses" so when you see this spelling you are seeing the language as he wrote it. Throughout 1918 and 1919 he wrote 64 episodes, each beginning:

PERSONS
Stories And Incidents
Of Old Boston
and the Old Days
By the Writer

He would then conclude each episode with memorable closing lines such as:

"Ditto Next Week"
"Next Week Again"
"Something Else Next Time"

Sometimes the closing was more flamboyant,

"Right at this point, we find we have "overdrawn" on our space account, so we will squirt some embalming fluid into the rest of the yarn to keep it from spoiling, and will give it to you the next time"

Many, but not all, of those 64 articles are a part of this compilation. A few of those tales written in 1918 and 1919 were not relevant to the story of Boston. Maybe I can find a use for them another time. Some stories are as much about Sam as they are about Boston, but they will give you a feel for both "The Writer" and the time and place in which the story occurs. Thus, this narrative is built around Konkel's writing with additional research to support and document his recollections of Old Boston and the area. However, on occasion, I believe Konkel's 30-year-old remembrance of events fails him and I have noted such cases and provided documentation. Sometimes, I have moved selected individual items from the sequence in which Konkel presented the story in 1918 and 1919 to help with the flow of this compilation. To emphasize when we are using Konkel's writing we will use a font similar to the one used in his paper in 1918. A sample is provided below:

If you see this font, it is Sam Konkel's writing.

These stories, tucked away in my hometown library and museum combined with additional news stories and clippings mentioned bring you the true story of gunfights and adventures of this short-lived Wild West town.

The goal of this project is twofold, first, to tell the story of Boston and second to celebrate frontier newspaperman Sam Konkel. His words within these pages do both. I hope you enjoy the story of this place, Old Boston, Colorado, as much as I have.

The Springfield Herald office in 1913 (far left) as it looked
when Sam Konkel returned to the newspaper business in Springfield, Colorado.[2]

"Our papers, our little country papers, seem drab and miserably provincial to strangers; yet we who read them, read in their lines the sweet, intimate story of life."

– William Allen White, *Emporia Gazette*, 1916

Sam Konkel was born March 30, 1853, the 7th of 14 children in Adams County, Indiana and was educated in the rural schools of Page County, Iowa. At various times he worked as a farmer, teacher, printer and newspaperman. His daughter, Laura, writes about her dad,

"When his brothers Will, Joe and Dave came visiting there was more political and religious discussions than anything else. Conversation was lively, but seldom dwelt on the past. I was the hapless 'referee' to many of these discussions and I must say these men were well educated and extremely well informed on any subject. The only really heated argument I remember about their past youth, was on the subject of Grandmother Konkel – did she or did she not smoke a pipe? Uncle Joe and Dad insisted she did and Uncle Will was just as insistent she did not. Uncle Dave abstained from the vote. Both Dad and Uncle Joe said she

smoked a corncob pipe and they often smoked with her when they came in working from the fields."[3]

At the age of 34, in the year 1887, Sam came to the east end of Las Animas County, Colorado, and established the *Western World* as one of two newspapers brought in to promote the now extinct town. The follow clippings document the maiden issue of Konkel's Boston newspaper adventure in March of 1887, as well as provide a reference to a "spicy paper" in 1888, one year into the paper's publication.[4] [5] [6]

> This week we are in receipt of the *Boston World*, Vol. 1, No. 1, a bright, newsy paper, published and edited by S. M. Konkel, at Boston, Colo.

> S. M. KONKEL, formerly of this county, is now publishing a paper, *The Western World*, at Boston, Las Animas county, Colorado, and seems to have caught the spirit of frontier newspaper men.

> We are in receipt of "The Western World" an eight column folio published in Boston, Colorado, and find it quite a spicy paper.

The story of Old Boston, Colorado is typical of many old west stories. The events there were colorful and violent, and it has a large and equally bright cast of characters. The critical link to the Boston,

Colorado, story is Sam Konkel. After leaving Boston he ran the paper in Lyons, Kansas and later taught in Indiana. During the time in Indiana he met his future bride, Clara Mae Simmons. He returned to Southeast Colorado in 1913 as editor of the *Springfield Herald* and ran the newspaper until he sold it in 1930 at the age of 77. While at the *Springfield Herald*, Konkel wrote many times about pioneer days, but did not actually begin the series containing information about Boston until 1918.

Left: Young-Sam Konkel when he was editor of the Boston World
Right: Sam Konkel, "The Writer" of these 1918-1919 recollections
of the Wild West town of Boston Colorado.[7]

He began thinking about these write ups shortly after buying the *Springfield Herald* in 1913. In the January 9, 1914 issue of the *Springfield Herald* he writes: The editor believes the most interesting period in Baca County's history is right now; but the old days had more thrilling events crowding one into another, and sometime in the not very distant future the Herald will recall some of those events by a write up of those old days- mostly in the way of a write up of old Boston, which at the time was the principal theater of thrilling events in the county, and the largest town the county has ever had.[8]

Konkel frequently refers to himself as the "The Writer," and the moniker is used throughout the series about Old Boston and the old days. The term is not unique to Konkel. It is fairly common to see the term, "The Writer," used by old time newspaper editors as when referring to something they wrote. His experience is first hand, his recollections critical to the history of old Baca County and his writing provides a new and unique view of life in an old west boom town.

In spite of the violence engulfing the town during its brief existence, he weaves a charming levity through the stories in the surviving newspaper accounts. He'd been recruited by the Boston town founders to bring a newspaper to the booming frontier town and became the key to preserving the history of this place.

The following stories about himself written eleven months into the series introduce you to the charming wit of Sam Konkel and help sets the stage for the story of "That famous ol' town," Boston, Colorado.

One on the Writer

It was way back in the fall of 1886, -- and the month was September, and the state was Kansas, and the county was Morton, though it strikes us that at the time it was Seward, afterward made into Morton, Stephens, Seward.

There was no Boston at that time, old or young, and old Baca County was a wild and weary waste -- and really didn't exist at all. While in Morton County there was only one town, called by the glowing term of Sunset.

At the beginning of our story, we were temporarily quartered at Great Bend. A brother of the writer had braved the wrath of the prairie-dogs and coyotes, and owls and rattlesnakes, in the springtime, so we thought to come out and look things over a little.

Now there was one thing in making that western trip that we hadn't taken into consideration -- the difference in elevation, and the consequent possible difference in climate.

Tin Lizzies[1] weren't much in evidence at that time, so we hitched one horse up to one buggy and started pell-mell for the Promised Land.

At the starting point it was hot enough to boil eggs in the noonday sun, so of course, all we needed in the way of raiment for the journey was something to keep the sun and dust off, and for that we took one of those old-fashioned, long tail summer dusters, made of cheesecloth one layer deep.

---

[1] Tin Lizzie is a term originally used as a nickname for early Ford cars, especially the Model T.

That was bully for the first days of the journey, but as we were gradually scaling those western heights the days grew milder and milder until the zenith of mildness was reached, and it began to go the other way.

Over in what is now Seward County Kansas were then two towns, Springfield and Fargo. At the latter of these famous old towns for county seat honors we made our headquarters for the last night (almost) of the journey, and in the morning started out on the wind-up of the last sixty miles.

The road from Fargo to Hugo, now Hugoton, was sandy, so with our now somewhat jaded horse and buggy traveling was somewhat slow, and it was maybe 1:30 pm when we got to Hugo, and maybe 2:00 or better when we started on the last half of the day's trip.

At Hugo they told us to keep the south road, as it would be less sandy, and that about ten miles east of Sunset it would cross the river and come into the other road, but that it would grow dimmer, and we'd have to watch close especially where it turned off to cross the river.

It was cloudy at noontime, and probably when fifteen miles of the last thirty were reeled off it began to rain; and in the language of slang eloquence, it was getting to be rotten cold.

The shades of night began to fall along with the falling of the rain, and when darkness was on we found ourselves without a road, without a compass, without any protection except that gauzy duster, and without any knowledge of where we were at.

Of course, it was useless to call for help, so we ‑‑ meaning the horse and buggy, kept pegging away until there was no longer any road to peg on. Then the three of us held a council of war, and I decided it were time to meander towards the river and try and outflank the forces of darkness by getting onto the road on the other side.

We drove probably half a mile to the river, found a place to get the three of us down the bank and then one of us pulled off his shoes and stockings ‑‑ socks to more properly wade across to make sure the other two wouldn't get into a hole and drown.

Finding the path was clear, meaning there was no hole to drown in, we drove across, rehabilitated our tender pedals, and then led the horse and buggy northward thinking we would stand a better chance of finding the road than they would.

We finally, to our great relief and satisfaction, found the road, one of us got in the buggy, and all started west. We neglected to say that the rain had temporarily ceased, but we hadn't driven far when it began to fall harder than ever, and "rotten cold" then was no name for it.

After getting on the road we would drive a while and stop and wonder, and then drive a while and stop and wonder again. etc. etc.

Right at this point, we find we have "overdrawn" on our space account, so we will squirt some embalming fluid

into the rest of the yarn to keep it from spoiling, and will give it to you the next time.[9]

One on the Writer Continued

The why of our stopping to wonder was whether it was safe to drive farther? We guessed there were three or four houses in the town, but it was getting to be late and if the lights were out and they were gone to bed we might drive right through the town[2] and not know it; and it is a case of that kind the next morning that we couldn't tell where we were or which way to go.

Probably a half dozen times we stopped and then risked another drive, thinking it possible that just one more drive would bring us within sight of the house lights.

It was probably 10 o'clock when we finally decided not to take any further risks. The rain was falling steadily, and our teeth were chattering reg'lar old-ager style.

After deciding to camp right there for the night we turned that horse and buggy right about face-- the direction the rain and wind were going, and said to the horse –

**"Please make yourself at home and
just as comfortable as you can."**

Then we took up the cushin and put it over us as a partial protection against the elements, and sat there and

---

[2] NOTE: He uses the term 'town' a couple of times to reference where his brother lived but there was no town there until November 1886.

shook and shook and shook, and teeth chattered and chattered and chattered, sometimes getting a snatch of fitful
sleep, but most of the time wondering how much longer it
would be til morning.

The rain after a while ceased falling, but it grew colder
as the night advanced, and of course, the shaking and chattering increased with the coldness.

After ages of this sort of camp life--probably after
coming out of one of those fitful sleeps, we could see a
difference in the horizon in the direction we were headed,
and knew that reinforcements in the way of dawn were at
hand.

Then when it was sufficiently light we turned that
horse and buggy once more right about face, and found
ourselves just at the foot of quite an upland slope.

Maybe we had already passed the town so anxiously we
drove to the top of the slope, when behold, there was the
great city -- not over half a mile from where we decided
to put up for the night.

We drove on to the town and then four miles out to
where our brother had unconditionally surrendered to the
charms of the country, where the man and the beast and
the buggy all put up for a good warm breakfast.

Big head? -- We never know before what it meant,
and the beastly thing stayed with us until the morning of
the next day.

That's all -- except that by the experience we learned
the difference between a low altitude and a high one.[10]

The Return: Sidewalks of Old Boston

Now we will have the sidewalks - see ordinance. This time the city has the contract and will put down the walks if the citizens fail to do so. Sixty days and we will be the only new town except for Lamar in eastern Colorado, with complete sidewalks. We will have another jubilee then. – *Western World* August 2, 1888.

Jas. D. Newton Saturday brought in the first load of native lumber that has found its way to our town. Dr. Brown ordered the lumber for sidewalks. It s made from hard pitch pine about ten miles south of Troy and sells there at $18.00 per thousand feet. - *Western World* August 19th, 1888.

To have real sidewalks in those days was something to holler about. The town wasn't two years old, so the sidewalks were really a wonderful achievement, and Boston of course was pretty well "blowed up" over it.

The walks we believe were eight feet wide and extended four blocks on Main Street and two blocks on 9th Avenue.

The city put down the sidewalks. We presume some of the lot owners paid for the walks collected as payment on that lumber.

In case the parties were to wait for their money till collected as taxes, on the lots, we are not presuming the lumber was ever paid for, as the town and the whole country went to the dogs the next spring, the good people not stopping about such little things as paying their taxes before going.

The writer left the country in May of 1889. At the time sidewalks were still there -- as standing (laying or lying) monuments to the industry and enterprise of the good new town; or shall we say as a satire on the stranded hopes and ambitions of those who just a few days before had seen the star of their destiny in the west and had moved to carve an empire out of the country to which the star led them. And of course, old Boston was all there at the time.

Fifteen years later "The Writer" rode down the Main street of old Boston and do you know, the first thing we thought of was those sidewalks -- and they were gone -- everything was gone.

On Nov. 1887, the Boston city council solemnly ordained an ordinance entitled --

"To prevent Removal of Town Property."

But here in the face of that ordinance, solemnly ordained, all the hooks, ladders and buckets belonging to the town were gone, the sidewalks were gone -- and the whole durned town was gone.

What had become of the hooks, ladders, and buckets? What had become of the sidewalks? What had become of the town? And the people -- where were all the people?

The thing that probably impressed us most as we rode into and stopped in the center of that old town was the awful stillness.

Of course we knew before riding into the town that everything was gone, but the feeling of that awful stillness in the center of that town was as if the good people of that good old town had met with some nihilating world catastrophe, and all its people were then sleeping beneath what was once its lively thoroughfares.

But the sidewalks -- bless your sweet life, we never did learn what happened to them, we will let them rest.

Something else next week[11]

Chapter 2: The Haystack Massacre

"Word from Stevens County says that the gang who killed Sheriff Cross and posse of Stevens in July 1888 are now under arrest. The murder created intense excitement through the western part of the state at the time, having grown out of the Hugoton-Woodsdale county seat war"

-*Lawrence Daily Journal*, Nov 1888

The bloody county seat wars of Kansas were very much on the minds of those settling Boston and rest of the southeast Colorado boom towns in 1886 -1887. Konkel recalls his meeting with Frank Jennings of the Atlantis Town Company,

"Frank stated that we didn't want to repeat the experience of Woodsdale and Hugoton and Richfield and Frisco, over in Kansas. That is, we didn't want any county seat fights."[12]

The occurrence of an event known as the Haystack Massacre is widely documented since Konkel's writing of the event in 1918. His perspective is close to the event in time and he likely met some of the participants as he frequently was in railroad meetings with town leaders of both Hugoton and Woodsdale. There is no doubt this event influenced the early settlement of Southeast Colorado. Konkel describes his remembrance,

Some County Seat Fights

On our side of the state line the county seat fights were strategic rather than sanguinary, the bickerings and verbal lance play of the press of the different towns bidding for the county seat honors constituting the principal war tragedies between the towns.

We spoke often of the desire of the Boston Town Company to avoid over on this side the sanguinary conflicts between the towns on the other side of the line that were rivals for county seat honors.

Richfield and Frisco, Morton County were three miles apart and one was a dead duck that failed to land first on the home base.

There are all kinds of scraps and shooting scrapes between the towns, but we believe there are no obituaries as a result of them.

As we recall it, the town of Richfield was shot up a few times in the stilly hours of the night, presumably by cow boys. At one time, Richfield was given a tip that Frisco was coming in mass to carry off the ballot box. Sometime in the night a score or more of the Friscoans on horseback halted in the south part of town ⸗ seeming to smell a mice that everything wasn t right.

And it wasn t ⸿ for them. In the midst of their parlay some over-anxious Richfielder couldn t hold himself any longer and then banged away at them. The Friscoans then fired a few times promiscuously at nothing like Braddock s Army[3], and then beat it.

As quick as they could get there the Richfielders ran out into the street and turned loose the repeating Winchesters. Probably all together 150 or 200 shots were fired. Providentially for the parties concerned there was no one brought down and consequently no funerals resulted from the night's escapade.

The Butchery in No Man s Land[4]

Practically every county in Western Kansas had its county seat fight and tragedies in many cases rivaling the free-soil tragedies of the '50-60' in the eastern part of the state.

It was the free-soil days following the repeal of the Missouri Compromise gave to the state the name of "Bleeding Kansas" and when the free-soil fight was over the "bleeding" was actually carried on to the western part of the state through fights between the towns of most of the counties in their rivalries in landing the county seat plum. We shall here relate one of those bloody tragedies.

---

[3] Edward Braddock was a British officer and commander-in-chief for the 13 colonies during the actions at the start of the French and Indian War (1754–1763).

[4] No Man's Land or Neutral Strip is known today as the Oklahoma Panhandle.

Woodsdale and Hugoton in Stevens County were two such towns. Sam Woods was the droll wit and the genius of Southwestern Kansas, a lawyer by profession and a general all-around promoter of Sam Woods Enterprises.

Woodsdale was one of those enterprises started a few miles north of Hugoton, the challenge thus being for a fight to the finish and the devil take the hindmost.

The climax to the situation came down in what then was known as the neutral strip or No Man s land, which included what are now Beaver, Texas, and Cimarron counties. The "strip" was afterward attached to Oklahoma, cannibalism ceased, the powwows and Sun Dances were left off and No Man's Land took its place among the civilized nations of the earth, and has become prosperous and happy.

But the story. We believe the trouble started on Election Day, and probably a kidnapped ballot box figured into the program. A warrant was sworn out for one of the Woodsdale outfit, a Hugo Deputy Marshal or Sheriff endeavoring to serve the warrant. The party wanted, thought the climate would be more congenial down in No Man s Land, and so they hiked it thence, with the deputy and a posse of Hugo avengers hot on their trail. Then Woodsdale organized a counter posse and started out for the scalps of the Hugo parties also ambulating to the sunny land of the neutral strip, where law knew no court and order knew no law.

All day and maybe all of another day the Woodsdale posse hunted for the Hugo party -- probably hot on their trail when, late at night, they lay down by the side of a haystack to a await the morning. It was about sun up in the morning when they were awoken from their peaceful slumbers by Hugo posse.

The first thing was to disarm them even down to their pocket knives. Then they were stood up in a line seven poor defenseless hapless Woodsdale boys, standing in line with their hands tied back of them – under the shadow of an endless night.

By lot one of the Hugo parties was designated to put out the lights of each of those seven boys.

"Ready Take Aim Fire" and one of the boys entered the endless night.

"Ready Aim Fire" and another Woodsdale boy came to the end of his earthly career.

And so was dropped the third, fourth, the fifth and the sixth.

The last one was a boy in age as well as in appearance maybe 16 years old. The practitioner slowly raised his gun, took aim, hesitated and then said ⸚

"I can t shoot him"

"By ⸗⸗⸗ I can shoot him,"   said the deputy; and he took up the gun and dropped the boy.

Story continued next week[13]

The Butchery Continued

To make sure their work was complete and that there would be no afterclaps, the Hugoites rolled the bodies right side up and kicked them, and there being no signs of life they mounted their steeds and rode back to civilization on the Kansas side of the state line.

We believe it was the next day when a boy, almost dead from the loss of blood, exposure and starvation, was found some distance from Springfield[14], Seward county, Kansas, next county east of Stevens, slowly and painfully dragging himself toward the town.

It was the nineteen-year old boy that the deputy dropped at the hay stack. He was rolled over and given the kicking test along with the others. He was conscious, knew what was going on, and knowing that a sign of life meant instant death, he played the game of being dead and got away with it.

We never learned anything further of the boy, but supposed he was nursed to recovery, and probably is living today. Anyway, he lived to tell the story of the foul murders in No Man's Land and who the Hugo parties were that did the killing.

About that time the whole west was breaking up--everybody moving away. The case was called and tried a number of times, but in the prejudiced state of mind of the few remaining it was impossible to find a jury that would convict, and the case was finally thrown out of court.

Sam Woods himself was the last victim of those old-time Stevens County tragedies. It was some time after the

county seat fight was over, and we believe his killing resulted from civil or criminal cases, disconnected from county
seat matters, though the enmities growing out of the old
town fights may have had something to do with it.

He was living in Woodsdale, when one night someone called him to the door, and when he appeared they
shot him dead in the doorway.

Because of its unusual features, we have digressed somewhat from the purpose of these old-time write-ups, the
stories of which we intended entirely for Baca County, and
mostly for old Boston itself, to relate this one story of
Stevens County. We shall consequently relate no more
Kansas Stories, except as they are directly related to our
own county and people.[15]

Chapter 3: Before Boston

"The only remarkable statement yet made concerning the man recently found dead west of here, is that he is not a member of a Colorado town company. On with the boom."

-*The Ashland Weekly Journal*, 1887

It is an understatement to say the complete story of Old Boston, Colorado has never been told. No foundations are left of any buildings and few details of the old town have been told except for the brief retelling of one or two stories. Included in the usual story told of the old town is how a feud between a storekeeper and a cow boy led to a vendetta against the storekeeper by the cow boy's friends, with the said return of the cow boys leading to the siege of the town.

In April 1889, the news of this siege was in papers coast to coast ranging from the Baltimore Sun[16] to the Los Angeles Times.[17] Just as quickly as the town rose from the prairie in November 1886, the citizens abandoned the town in the spring of 1889. A few brave souls stayed on through 1892 but it was in effect finished by April 1889. By 1913, when Al Jennings of Oklahoma outlaw fame penned his autobiography, Boston, Colorado, could no longer be found on a map. In his book, the story of the town only received a few paragraphs even though the Jennings clan was part of the Boston Town Company which was pushing the startup of Old Boston.

They raced many other town companies to the Colorado prairie in an attempt to build a town which could become the county seat and catch the railroad during the town boom days of Southeastern Colorado in 1886 -1887. There is some debate on the actual start date for Old Boston but the various versions agree it was in the month of November 1886 when the first stakes were driven.

>   *"Several men stopped to stay overnight with the Simeon Konkel* (Sam Konkel's brother) *family. In this company, there was a Mr. Hughes, Judge Jennings, known as the "Silver Tongued Orator" and his two sons Al and Ed. The Jennings were all lawyers. They were going two miles south and eight west of the Konkel home to lay out the town-site of Boston. On November 16, 1886, the town-site was surveyed and staked out, thus establishing the town of Boston, Colorado."*[18]

By early spring 1887, Boston had a thriving downtown, and over 70 houses built to provide a windbreak from the ever-present prairie wind. While nervously eyeing the county seat wars of Kansas, 15 miles to the east and the odd lawless rule of order 15 miles to the south in No Man's Land, Boston's town founders established what Sam Konkel called "The Utopian City of the Plains." A remarkable cast of characters brought their dreams and fortunes hoping to expand both. This influx of people led to a real-life script which turned Boston into one of the wildest little towns on the new frontier. The brief existence played out a turbulent and often violent existence for three years and then as quickly as the town was, it wasn't.

Every new boom town of that era had at least one newspaper promoting it and Boston had two. Both, Konkel's *Western World* and George Daniel's *Boston Banner* were in the business of promoting the city. The newspaper header for the *Western World* boldly proclaimed,

"Land for the Landless and Homes for the Homeless"[19]

Ads promoting Boston from the March 8, 1888 *Western World* used phrases such as, "Hub of the Universe," "The Utopian City of the Plains," and "Railroads a Moral Certainty." Certainly the town founders were banking on the coming of the railroad and gaining the county seat, both factors which had not yet occurred.[20]

BOSTON,

Las Animas County,

COLORADO!

-*Th Utopian City of the Plains!*-

THE HUB OF THE UNIVERSE.

Railroad and Commercial Center.

It is on a DIRECT LINE with all the county seat towns in the southern tier of counties in Kansas, with Trinidad and the GREAT COAL FIELDS directly west, thus making several east and west

RAILROADS A MORAL CERTAINTY:

It now has DAILY MAIL to Richfield, Granada, Lamar, and Trinidad. The county is unsurpassed for the quality and fertility of its soil, and its Pure, SOFT water. Its farming lands are in a compact body, with long slopes and large flats and valleys stretching as far as the eye can reach. Boston has a BRASS BAND of Professional Players whose MUSIC makes the heart of every citizen swell with honest pride.

A $10,000 HOTEL

now built—3 stories, 45 x 52 feet— the Grandest and Biggest of any in the southwest.

Promotional ad for Boston in the *Boston World*, March, 1888.

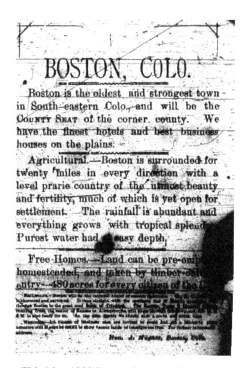

This May 1888 Boston Banner ad promoted
Boston as the new county seat of the corner county.

The promoters of this new frontier were doing an effective job of selling the town back east as shown in ads and news reports from towns such as Ashland, Greensburg, and Winfield, Kansas. In the spring of 1887 there many conversations about the exodus of these Kansas citizens.

"Already the roads are lined with covered wagons –from twenty five to fifty passing through this place daily. The frontier has already reached the western line of the state and is lopping over onto Colorado."[21]

Ads such as this in the August 1887, *Greensburg (KS) Rattler* did nothing to deter the desire to move to Colorado.[22]

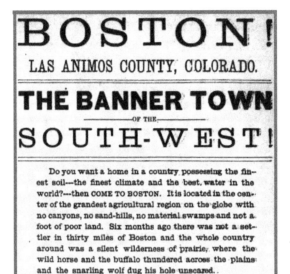

They did have their work cut out for them with competition from other town companies. Seventeen towns popped up on the Southeast Colorado prairie in 1886 and 1887. Everyone it seems was part of some town building effort with each town company trying to build the next great city on the Colorado prairie.

The First White Man Met

It was after we had licked the platter on the morrow after the first night this way over the Kansas-Colorado line that a man on horseback rode up to our camp and asked if we had seen anything of a bunch of horses.

We answered that we hadn t, but that a bunch of wild horses about an hour before had galloped out of sight towards the West.

"That s them," He said - "they re my horses. I ve been following them for two days. I camped just over the hill there last night."

The man had a couple of blankets, a raincoat, and prob- ably some chuck in his pockets or wrapped in with his bundles, but there was nothing in sight, so out of the com- passion of our civilized hearts we said,

"We ve had our breakfast, but we have some flapjacks left and some coffee and smear stuffs and if you like you can help yourself and welcome."

The man ate heartily and talked freely, more about his horses than anything else. After getting away with rem- nants of our breakfast he mounted and rode westward after the wild brutes he called his horses.

The fellow was Henry Savoy whose history was woven into the after events of the east-end settlement, and whose career ended in tragedy at Old Boston. We shall have occasion to refer to him hereafter.

Thirty Miles from Water

It was noon on the same day. Like the foolish virgins who failed to take oil along for their lamps, we at the end of second day noon found ourselves without any water for either ourselves or our horses on the then nameless North Fork of the Great American desert.

A ride down the creek for a few miles found nothing, while a short distance up the creek found a hole with water remaining in the old cow tracks.

We strained that through a sand sieve, made coffee of it, and called it good. The horses also drank of the stuff that we dipped up for them and put in a bucket.

Two miles north of the creek was located the future Konkel ranch, on which we camped that night and then drove back to Richfield, Kans., thirty miles away to get water for ourselves and horses.

Incidentally, what the writer was after was to get near the center of what might be a future county ⸗ cut off from Las Animas County, which the county was then.

The location we found was fifteen miles from the east line and seventeen from the south line which would be the center of an ordinary eastern county.

Frank Jennings

It was along in July, and the writer was on the top of a wall laying sod for what was intended for a barn when two rigs containing four people each drove up, they said people wanted to know a little of everything about the country and especially as to where they could find a township corner.

As was surmised at the time that bunch of fellows was looking for a town site. They drove back to Richfield, but about a month afterwards the famous town of Boston was projected and the necessary steps taken to procure the land for the town-site purposes.

Richfield, Kansas, thirty miles to the east, was our post office and the nearest trading station.

Along in September a young smooth-faced, intelligent and rather pleasant looking fellow called at our room at the Aurora Hotel where we always put up when in Richfield, and introduced himself.

The young fellow was Frank Jennings of the famous Jennings family, the boys of which afterwards in Oklahoma became train robbers and general outlaws, and were finally run down and served time in the pen.

Frank led off at once on the mission of the call. He was secretary of the Atlantis Town Company. They had started a town over in Colorado three miles west of us. Intended to call it Atlantis, but changed it to Boston.

> Citizens of Ashland have incorporated
> and obtained charters for the following
> enterprises: Ashland State Bank, cap-
> ital $50,000; Winton & Deming State
> Bank, capital $60,000; Ashland Build-
> ing and Loan Association, capital $1,-
> 000,000; Lincoln Mortgage and Trust
> Company, capital $100,000; Ashland
> Concrete Manufacturing Company, cap-
> ital $5,000; Humbar Town Company,
> capital $12,500; Albany Town Company
> capital $10,000; Boston Town Company,
> capital $10,000. Where is there anoth-
> er town no older than Ashland that can
> show up such a record.—Herald.

Throughout this narrative, you will see references to the Atlantis Town Company. This may be a point which Konkel did not remember correctly. It is likely they were going to name it the Atlantis Town Company. There are mentions of both town company names in various places, but the notice in the April 1, 1887 Lexington, Kansas paper shown above indicates the town company which was created was actually the Boston Town Company.[23]

Frank stated that we didn't want to repeat the experience of Woodsdale and Hugoton and Richfield and Frisco, over in Kansas. That is, we didn't want any county seat fights, and Boston being located, the company would give us certain interests in the town if we would join them.

The arrangements were made. We would join the town in the spring and start a newspaper -- in consideration of certain interests; and this we did in the March following.[24]

The Founding of Boston

In the midst of a blizzard in November 1886, the first tents were pitched in Boston and the first lumber arrived on the ground. Colorado style, the snow flurry was soon over and in a few days, a lot of carpenters and helpers were busy on a lot of business buildings grouped about a common center.

In those days the wells all over the west were dug, and almost immediately upon the landing of those Boston Pilgrims, a well was started at the intersection of the two main streets of the town; and it was along in the spring before the well was completed and a windmill installed.

So rapidly were the building operations pushed that by the first of March seventy houses, mostly businesses, were built, and Boston began to take the appearance of a real town.

Boston wasn't quite the first in the east end -- as this part of Las Animas County was then called. Butte City was started in June 1886; but we believe that less than half a dozen houses were built there when it was abandoned and the houses moved over to Minneapolis, started a few miles west of it in the summer of 1887.

A few days after Konkel's arrival at the new town in the spring of 1887, he was talking to a group of prospective nesters when a small faced old gentleman, standing nearby, asked, "Are you Mr. Konkel?"

"Yes"

"I am Judge Jennings, I've heard a lot about you, and I am glad to meet you," he said as they shook hands. That was the introductory meeting with the elder Jennings.[25]

"Railroads A Moral Certainty."

–Sam Konkel, 1888

Bringing the railroad to Boston and southeast Colorado was the task most on the minds of the Boston town founders outside the efforts to gain the county seat. Often the term "road" was used when discussing the coming of the railroads. When you see this term later, it is referring to the railroads. Various justifications were provided for bringing the railroad to Southeast Colorado, such as,

>*"From Trinidad will go out fuel supply (coal) and lumber merchandise." Carriso Springs will be a shipping point on a large scale for the Prairie Cattle Company. The quarries at Carriso will furnish a stone, more easily worked for flagging and building than any I ever saw."*[26]

The coming of the railroads was also a reminder of the hostilities between various towns in Western Kansas and Eastern Colorado. The *Seward County Courant* reports in September of 1887,

>*"The meeting of the representative citizens of Seward, Stevens and Morton counties, and eastern Colorado, at*

Woodsdale, a week from last Monday, was well attended from the counties named. It was not intended at this meeting to build a railroad, but to agree upon some plan to secure those that are soon to be built in western Kansas. A farce of a meeting was some weeks ago held at Hugoton, and after those present filled themselves up with Hugoton whisky, they enthused to such an alarming extent that it was decided to build a railroad at once. Officers were elected, a charter filed with the secretary of state, when in fact the entire number of projectors for this con-templated road do not represent twenty-five thousand dollars. The public is becoming sorely disgusted with this method of booming a town or county. The meeting at Woodsdale was altogether for another purpose. There are three competing lines of important railroads headed for southwestern Kansas, and the object of the successful meeting held at Woodsdale was to arrive at some understanding as to the best methods to employ in order to secure these lines of road through the counties named in the cities of Springfield, Woodsdale, and Richfield in Kansas as well as Boston, Colorado. The meeting was harmonious throughout. Cheering speeches were made, the several committees appointed and everything that could possibly be done to complete an organization for the purpose of securing the railroads that are to soon reach western Kansas. The representative men from the several towns and localities interested have gone into this work with a unity of action, and we can expect much good as the result of this meeting."[27]

Railroads were a rallying cry for these 1880s boom towns. An ad by the Boston Company in the Greensburg, Kansas *Rattler* in 1887 proclaimed the following:[28]

RAILROADS !

"Westward the star of Empire moves" and so do the Rail Roads. There are at the present time no less than five roads heading directly for Boston and as we are directly in the line of their objective destination they cannot possibly pass us without making a curve greatly to their detriment. Aside from these considerations we have the assurance of two that their surveying corps will be in Boston in less than two weeks. We are assured of the fact, that in less than six months the iron horse will be dashing through our valleys, eating up the forests and drinking the rivers dry, making Boston the Kansas City of the West.

The town leaders when not in Boston spent much of their time away attending railroad meetings in Trindad and Lamar, Colorado, Richfield, Kansas, and other locations. These meetings often referenced building "roads" which at that time referred to railroads. These meetings also revolved around enticing investment and finalizing the route for a railroad. There is evidence the railroads were actively investigating those possibilities, so it wasn't always just something dreamed up by the town promoters. Such news of railroad representatives visiting southeast Colorado boom towns was common and the enthusiasm of such meetings raised to a fever pitch. Almost daily reports told of the certainty of the railroad coming to town.

> The Boston World came out in red last week, exultant over railroad news. Boston is destined to become' one of the railroad centers of south-eastern Colorado.

Railroad Excitement[29]

The *Trinidad Daily Citizen* reported,

"J. L. Palmer representing the Rock Island road, has been at Boston for a day or two and a large and enthusiastic meeting was held last night to hear his propositions. We will give them next week in full. Suffice to say now that a Rock Island survey will pass through Boston within fifteen days. It is quite likely, too, that the road will be completed from here to Trinidad before another half a twelvemonth – **Boston Banner***"* [30]

Whether there was any accuracy to stories of the railroad coming or not most newspapers drew and printed maps of the proposed railroad maps to show their citizens the railroad was coming. The following map was printed in many issues of the 1887 and 1888 *Trinidad Daily Citizen.*

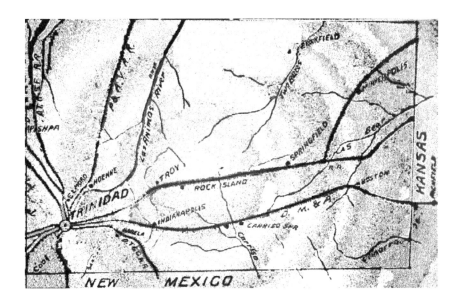

Konkel does not write extensively about the railroad efforts, but he and other Boston officials were at many if not all of the railroad meetings held in Western Kansas and Trinidad. Town founders knew this would be a key factor in which towns survived. His paper, *"The Western World,"* pushed the inevitable coming of the railroad with the motto we began this chapter with, **"Railroads A Moral Certainty"**[31]

Konkel's brief discussion of the railroad in the 1918 -1919 write-ups is as follows,

Railroad Building

The two things of these old days that had the certainty of the sun rising and setting were rains and railroads. Every town in the east end had them – railroads, none less than two or three.

Among the roads that all of them had were the Rock Island, Santa Fe, Colorado and Southern, Denver and Gulf, M.K and T., B. T. and W. Wichita and Western, and others too numerous to here mention.

The B.T. W.The B.T. W.

The B. T. and W. Boston, Trinidad and Western was the most exploited of those old time sure thing railroads. It had its birth in Trinidad, but was really fathered by Judge J.D.F. Jennings, father of the afterwards notorious Jennings boys in connection with Albert Hughes, the president of the Atlantis Town Company.

A number of Trinidad financiers were in on the ground floor of the promoted enterprise, but the actual money put up was by Hughes himself.

Word was given out that the line was being promoted under the authority of the Rock Island by which it would be taken over as soon as graded.

Accordingly, the B.T. and W. company started a survey at the state line, and after about three weeks drove the last stake at the Trinidad end of the line.

The town fathers of these boom towns also attempted to establish rules of order for a civilized town with ordinances which limited the livestock running loose in town. They hoped such laws would bring a more civilized feeling to the town.

Ordinance No. 21.
Passed Feb. 27, 1883,
To repeal sec. 6 ordinance No. 1.
Be it ordained by the board of trustees of the town of Boston:
Section 1. That section 6 ordinance No.1 permitting the running at large of cattle horses and mules in the town in the day time is hereby repealed.
Sec. 2. This ordinance shall take effect and be in force at the expiration of five days after publication.

Another Boston Ordinance:
No more cattle, mules and horses running loose in the daytime.[32]

Konkel relates the following story about livestock running loose on the streets of Old Boston,

A Hog Ordinance

The Boston council was pretty good at passing metropolitan ordinances – they had Springfield skinned a mile, and Springfield had been doing pretty well. We quote the following: Last week according to ordinances solemnly ordained by the city council, the hogs of the city – or city hogs as the case may be, were surrounded and driven to the city caboose, there to remain in durance vile until costs were paid. Then in a day or two the owner of that "calaboose came along and wanted to know what in gehenna those pigs were doing in his house. He was wroth, but turned the pigs out with the admonition not to repeat the offense, or they'd get the eternal stuffing kicked out of them.

The hogs then went to bust up the city council presumedly to get a drink of water. In the catastrophe that followed the hogs were again impounded and will now be held on an indictment for contempt of court, and for disturbing the peace and quiet of the city while being arrested –. *Western World* Sep 22, 1888[33]

Chapter 5: A Few People in the Limelight

"This Boston town certainly lacked the culture and refinement of its New England namesake. Saloons, gamblers and painted women prevailed."

- Albert W. Thompson

More famous Wild West towns preceding Boston like Dodge City or Abilene produced legendary western characters such as Wyatt Earp, Bat Masterson and Wild Bill Hickok. No one in the Southeast Colorado boom era found such lasting fame. When Boston disappeared, everyone literally walked away and disappeared without a trace with the possible exception of the Jennings clan which later gained notoriety as outlaws in Oklahoma. Al Jennings, after leaving Boston, formed the Jennings gang of Oklahoma along with his brother Frank, Little Dick West and a couple of others. Jennings went on to acquire a bit of fame in Hollywood, but the others mostly left town never to be heard of again.

Boston had its own Billy the Kid who became city marshal at age 16…he just wasn't the more famous Billy the Kid. Konkel mentions a Bostonian named Lou Reeder who we will discuss in more detail later. He says Lou Reeder was raised by the "Jenningses" and was a trouble maker, Reeder is a mystery not only because of his role in the final siege of Boston, but like everyone else he disappears. He is never mentioned with the "Jenningses" after they go to Oklahoma and become outlaws. Others ranging from regulators for the large foreign owned cattle companies to speculators came to Boston to seek land and new opportunity.

There was little news about the women of Boston. In April of 1887, it was reported that Misses Anna and Josie Semma had left Richfield, Kansas to "secure some lots in that burg."[34] There is no additional detail as to the purpose of purchasing those lots. The November 25, 1887 edition of the *Trinidad Citizen* printed news from the *Boston Banner* that as many as twenty young ladies were proving up claims or had already done so.[35]

"There are more brave young ladies around Boston than any place in the west."

One of the more notable deaths in Boston not involving outlawry was that of Ed Jennings wife, Ettie also called Tena. One report indicates she passed from Typhoid fever. The following report from Coldwater, Kansas provides no cause,

"Death Has Done a Cruel Thing. No sadder event has happened at Boston than the recent death of Mrs. Ettie A. Jennings. She was taken ill on her way out here last week and was here but three days in a home she had craved to reach when the "pallid messenger of the inverted torch" beckoned her away. -- Boston,

Colo., Banner. Mrs. Jennings was the wife of Ed. Jennings, for-merly a resident of this county."[36]

A few reports show women in Boston starting businesses such as the one below:[37]

> Mrs. P. A. Hill went over to Boston this week to start a restaurrant and boarding house, and will feed the hungry Bostonians from now on.

You will see the Capanzky name later, but the hardy pioneer spirit is quite evident in Mrs. Capanzky as shown in the report below:[38]

> **FEMALE NERVE.**
>
> Probably a time of peace never furnished a more remarkable example of feminine energy and dauntless will than this:
>
> Mrs. Czapansky wanted a well on her mother's claim. Her husband was unable to dig it, being blind, and she went at it herself. Her two little boys did the work at the windlass while she dug and blasted below the surface. At a depth of fourty-seven feet she was rewarded by the discovery of a strong vein of the precious fluid.
>
> How many ladies in Colorado—in the universe—would undertake and carry to completion such a job? Shame on the strong man who after this does without a well on his farm.—Boston Banner.

The following summary is a composite of Konkel's recollections as well as newspaper reports which give us more detail on those who came to southeast Colorado to establish and settle in Boston in the late 1880s,

Right in line with those who brought or made fortunes here and lost them, might be mentioned those others whose prominence, business, characteristics, notoriety or achievements -- at the time or since has made or would make them interesting subjects in common conversation.

Albert Hughes

Albert Hughes would be the first on the list under any and all of the attributes here enumerated. But we will cover all of peculiarities of Hughes when discussing Tioga county and fortunes made and lost.

The Old Judge and his family

The Jenningses would come next to the bar -- partly from the reputation they bore, partly while in Boston from the reputation they made, and very largely from the notoriety they afterwards achieved.

Whatever else may be said of them, they were not fools for the want of brain capacity; but they afterward became fools because of a wrong direction of them.

Old Judge Jennings was a little of everything on top of ground -- a genius, a wizard, a diplomat, an orator, a doctor, a lawyer, and good many other things all in a bunch.

The old judge had the face of a weasel and the cunning of a fox. On top of it all he had brains, and controlled by those brains was a tongue that could be used to the dis-comfiture of anyone who attempted to cross his path -- when the crossing was the wrong way of the grain."

Judge J.D.F. Jennings[39]

As a public speaker, the judge was without peer in the southwest, unless an exception is made in the case of preacher Evans, who lived somewhere in the neighborhood of present day Konantz and whose sympathies by reason of his location were with Minneapolis - in the fight for the county seat. As an aside, as we shall not have occasion to again refer to Evans, it will suffice here to say that he was a speaker of the first water, and we believe a thoroughly upright man.

Living in the neighborhood of Minneapolis, he naturally cast his fortunes with that town and had he lived no doubt would have wielded a strong influence in the fight for the county seat honors.

He was diplomatic and fearless in what he championed and in his public addresses were along the lines of his convictions and the cause he championed.

On one occasion at Boston, he bearded the lion in his den in a speech favoring Minneapolis for the county seat - - that speech made all those Bostonians sit up and take notice.

We believe it was not more than a week or two after this that Evans was instantly killed by being hooked in the eye by a vicious cow.

When the news reached Boston of the fatality, it was Judge Jennings who said it was the best thing that could have happened to Boston, which was a compliment in line with what the North said when Stonewall Jackson was accidentally killed by his own troops.

The greatest fault in the traits of the Jenningses was their habit of bullying down the opposition. They were not quarrelsome in the sense of hunting trouble.

So long as you didn't directly cross their path, or wasn't particularly in their way to reach the desired end and you were with them, or even neutral, they gave you no direct occasion for a quarrel.

As means of achieving an end, they were consciousless and unscrupulous. With them, it was anyway to get there. They could be sociable, clever, pleasant and agreeable or they could turn either the butt or the muzzle of their guns and force their way; and what trouble they had in Boston was solely from this cause.

The Jenningses next week[40]

A Few People In the Lime Light.

The Jenningses Continued

It was a bright, sunshiny morning, and up at the old public well were, maybe half a dozen people. Something unusual seemed to be in the air, and something stirring at the old town well.

Indeed a scrap was developing. Bob Hambric by some means had gotten in bad with the Jenningses, and John Jennings was delegated to chastise and discipline said Hambric by handing him up a few.

John Jennings[41]

The writer had just gotten up and taken a look out the window when the entertainment began. John advanced, put his wrong foot forward, and swung with his right. But before it had time to land, Bob as he ducked, swung with his right and caught John some place about the sub-maxillaries, whereby said Jennings took up a new position on terra firma -- corresponding to the lay of the country.

That closed round one. Evidently John wasn't impressed with the showing he had made and thought he would stand a better chance with the butt of his gun. He made a swing with it, but Tom Hambric grabbed it from the rear, and held it as a contraband of war.

The insurgents then declared a truce, and in the language of Carnegie, the jig was up for that morning. It was three days before John would promise not to use his gun if given back to him, when he came again into possession of his little pet.

It was another bright balmy morning when there seems again to be something doing up at the old town well. This time the whole town seemed to be there, and Frank Jennings and Geo. Daniel were the central figures in a ring that had been formed roundabout.

There was a quarrel on between the Jenningses and Hughes. George, thinking that it was up to him to stand-in with the side that has a $ attached to it, proceeded through his paper to pour some hot shot into the old judge.

Thereupon the Jenningses held a council of war, to determine the counter offensive. Frank was charged to argue the case with Daniel; and in order that his argument would be effective in convincing George and turning him from the error of his ways, he provided himself with an unabridged pair of lead knucks.

Unlawyer like, Frank thus provided himself with the wrong text book to win the case. When the writer came on the scene, Frank was holding his knuck hand back of him, the knucks being so twisted that he couldn t further use them.

George s face was bleeding profusely from two or three blows from the knucks, and they were holding each other at arm s length neither apparently caring to reopen the argument.

At the beginning of the offensive, which was previous to our arrival, Lou Reeder-- a boy the Jenningses has raised, and Forney, afterwards Al, kept the crowd back at the muzzle of their guns. Lou, it was said, shoving his cocked gun against the breast of the innermost ones of the ring ordering them to stand back.

Frank, with the knucks bent down his hand, wasn't in shape to continue the drive, and George seeming to have had a plenty and willing to throw up the sponge and quit, they mutually backed away from each other and the enter-tainment was over for that time.

The Jenningses and "The President" (Albert Hughes), were sometimes at thick and sometimes thin, sometimes at outs and sometimes at ins. The old judge would come down the street one day and holding on to a lamp post, tell what "the president and I" were going to do; another day, hold-ing onto the same lamp post, he would tell what he was going to do to the "president" metaphysically speaking.

"The president and I" was his favorite theme. "The president and I" this and "the president and I" that. "The president and I" was the alpha and omega --the first and the last, in the judge's conversation, exclamations, and other forms of entertainments and activities.

Communicated.

Oct. 18th 1887.

MR. EDITOR: My time has been so continuously occupied since parting with you that I have positively had no time to write you, and even now I am sure my letter will not interest you.

I desire to say, first of all, that in all my travels I have never met a more generous and jolly set of people than the people of Trinidad and I will only forget them when I cease to have a memory.

The President and I had a very pleasant trip home ward and had a rare opportunity to study the country, the towns, and people along our route.

It is marvelous how rapidly the country is settling—How many new towns have sprung into existence in the last twelve months, and what a change has come over the agricultural districts.

Our favorite new town, Boston, is on a grand boom. She is just now full of speculators, capitalists and home seekers all anxious to invest in Boston.

In conclusion allow me to say that this end of the county will send to Trinidad an overwhelming majority for the entire Democratic ticket and that we all love THE CITIZEN.

THE JUDGE.

Judge Jennings: "The President and I"[42]

55

It was at Trinidad, and the board of County Commissioners were in session. Judge Jennings and Doc McCrory
had performed a post-mortem on one of Boston s unfortu-
nates who had died without making his will.

The charge for their services we believe was $40, but
may have been more. In any event, it was a clear case of
graft, and the commissioners refused to pay the bill.

Forney was selected as the attorney in the case, and as
we were afterwards informed, his arguments were a pistol
and vituperation.

The commissioners were not familiar with the Blacksto-
nian methods, and in the end Forney convinced them that
they were wrong, and they allowed the bill.

This information came second-hand, and it may be the
details were exaggerated, but there is no doubt that the
board allowed a bill for expert surgical services that might
as well have been performed on a dead cat.

The Jenningses Next Week[43]

A Few People in the Limelight

The Jenningses Continued

As to the activities of the Jenningses outside of the pale
of the law--as highwaymen, it isn't probable that they
were engaged in it while at Boston, making an exception of
one trip that Forney made through Texas at a time when
the Jenningses and everybody else were wondering where
the next dollar was coming from.

At this time the Jenningses particularly were all in-- didn't have between them enough pennies to make a Sunday school contribution; and to replenish their larder, Forney hired himself on a trip through Texas being gone about three months.

Forney was quite a sprinter, so it was given out that he was running races, and they were all betting that he would come back with money.

Al "Forney" Jennings[44]

He came back with money as they said he would, but how much nobody knew, and neither, of course, did any-body know how he got it. He may have gotten it by sprinting, but in view of the history they afterwards made for themselves in Oklahoma, it is just possible that he got it by some of the arguments afterward used in their Okla-homa experience.

This was the only time that any of them were absent from Boston outside of short trips to Trinidad and Denver except for one half a year when Frank was working in the county clerk s office in Trinidad.

Neither is it likely that the Jenningses were connected while at Boston with other people in the outlaw business. About the only stealing going on in the old east end was by a certain character who came to be known as "Billy the Kid," whom we will have occasion to notice later on.

Billy got into the horse (stealing) business, but while at it, went alone. The Neutral Strip was supposed to be headquarters for thieves, but as the Jenningses could be of little or no service to them, there was no particular reason why the swag should have been divided up, or that the Jenningses should have been taken in as partners. We think it consequently not probable that they were connected with any of the thieves at that time.

The history of the family in Oklahoma is pretty gen-erally known by both old timers and new timers. Ed was killed by a grandson of the famous General Sam Houston.[45] The killing was this way: John, Ed, and Forney--down there known as "Al", entered the side door of a saloon and opened fire on Houston, who was standing at the bar. When the smoke cleared away, Ed was dead, and John had an arm shot off.

The particular nature of the trouble with Houston we haven't learned. Houston, however, was a criminal lawyer. The Jennings boys were trying to work up a law business. In the absence of any certain information on the subject, it is probable that Houston was too much for them, as op-posing counsel, and it can be well surmised that the Jenningses tried to even things up by their old game of bluff and bulldozing and in this case happened to meet up with a man they couldn't work it on.

Shortly after the trouble with Houston, the boys, Frank and Forney, took to the highway business -- mostly in the way of train robberies, but were finally captured and served time in the pen -- we believe something over five years, though both were in for life.

After coming out of the pen the boys put their old lives back of them, returning to the scenes of their crimes to live it down.

Of course, it was a hard struggle, but they both stayed with it, and both have made good. Frank was married several years after coming out of the pen, and we presume is in the law business.

Forney -- Al -- well, he got married too, and has since made himself famous as a lawyer and a politician as he did as a criminal. He ran for district attorney at Oklahoma City, then ran for the Democratic nomination for governor, and both times made the other fellow and all the natives sit up and take notice.

That Forney is on Easy Street is evidenced by the fact that as a criminal attorney he commands fees anywhere from $1,000 to $10,000, and that as a public lecturer he probably commands from $100 to $500 per single engagements.

John continued in the law business, and we presume has done fairly well.

And the old judge. He lived to a very old age, and we believe only recently passed in his chips and had them cashed. He was a probate judge before coming here, and in Oklahoma succeeded in getting himself again elected as a probate judge.

In leaving the Jenningses for other topics, we would say of the old judge -- peace to his ashes and may he find less booze, less trouble, and more prosperity in his new home than he had in his terrestrial one

Something else Next Week.[46]

Lou Reeder

We are mentioning Lou here primarily for the reason that he was one of the factors in the final grand Boston round-up, and secondarily because in a way he was one of the characters of the old town.

If a biography of Lou were written, the first thing probably that would be chronicled would be the fact that he was raised by the Jenningses. We don't know where they picked him up, or the circumstances of their finding him, but as he seemed to be thoroughly domesticated it would seem they took him into the family in early childhood.

Of course being raised by the Jenningses carries its own significance. Lou was schooled in the art of carrying a big gun, and developed into somewhat of a threatener with the big gun-- apparently once and awhile just to show them.

We have already told how he and Forney kept the crowd back during the fight between Frank Jennings and Geo. Daniel, Lou shoving the muzzle of his cocked gun against the breast of some and commanding them to "stand back."

We'll mention one other gunplay of his. Sometime earlier in the day Forney and John told Lou that saloonkeeper Richards had said so and so about him. What the so and so was we don t now recall, but it doesn t matter anyway.

Along in the afternoon, Richards was leaning against the awning post on the sidewalk, when a voice back of him said--" did you say so and so about me"? Turning about on being thus accosted, Richards found himself looking down the barrel of Lou Reeder's gun.

Just then Forney and Ed came up and shoved Lou away, while Forney told him they were only joking about it and that Richards hadn t said anything.

As an illustration of Lou's idea of bulldozing his way through, he had been going with a certain widow of the town while another young blood by the name of Jack Fisher had also kept her company.

Of Jack we will have more to say when we come to the final town round-up.

Right here, having again" overdrawn" on our space account, we will have to do as we did last week-- squirt some embalming fluid into the rest of the story to keep it from spoiling and give it to you another time.[47]

Lou Reeder Continued

It was at a pow wow of the Philomathians[5] that a little incident of Lou and Jack and the widow occurred.

As stated, sometimes one of the boys and sometimes the other would give his attention to the widow, but on this occasion, Jack having brought her to doings properly, had the right of way.

And he did have the right of way as far as bringing the girl was concerned, but on attempting to continue the right of way for the return trip he was backed up by the knight errant Reeder, who just calmly walked up, disarmed the pair and walked off with the prize of contention.

We shall have Lou on the carpet again at the final windup of the town.[48].

---

[5] The Philomathean Society of the University of Pennsylvania is a collegiate literary society and claims to be the oldest continuously existing literary society in the United States. Philomathean is derived from the Greek philomath, which means "a lover of learning."

"The Colorado fever has struck some of our farmers who are only waiting for a sunny breeze from the south to start them on their journey."

-Medicine Lodge Cresset, 1887

The lure of free land and new opportunity attracted a mix of gunfighters, bartenders, lawyers, doctors, and ruffian scum along with the average homesteader to Boston, Colorado. J. R. Austin says,

> *"Low characters naturally gravitated in this direction where they would be in less danger of the law. Peaceable men were sometimes forced to become murderers through association with the lawless element who were thrown in their midst. Questions were not asked of their past."*[49]

Various newspaper accounts provide support for Austin's view. Many who came to Boston had no idea about the criminal element they were about to encounter. The events of this old town documented by Sam Konkel provide insight on how mixing of settlers with this lawless element was about to change all of their lives. Konkel was prophetic as he discusses the events of Boston and its citizens being as interesting as or more interesting than anything a fiction novelist might imagine.

Fortunes Made and Fortunes Lost

The fortunes in those days that were brought and dropped, or made and dropped, would make interesting reading in any wild-west fiction that might be written.

Even our town of Boston had some of these unlucky ones-- men who came with fortunes in front of them, and went away with fortunes, "Back of them."

Albert Hughes was one of those mortals. He was a shrewd business manager and was reputed to be worth $75,000. He was the president of the town company and the main spoke in the Boston Town Company, the Carrizo Town Company, the Albany Town Company, as well as Brookfield and Indianapolis, all towns of which he projected and mostly financed.

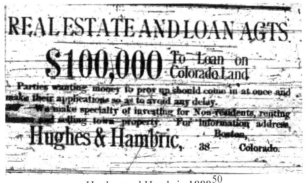

Hughes and Hambric 1888[50]

Hughes began his town building back in Kansas, Ashland being one of the chief ones he had helped build, and he had interests also in Meade Center at the time he went into the town building business in this corner of Colorado.

Ashland Clipper 1884[51]

He gradually disposed of his interests in those towns and salted his money down in the towns above mentioned; and got out of the country with anything from $2,000 to $6,000.

The Jennings family probably came here with $10,000. The old judge was vice president of the Boston Town Company and Frank the secretary. The old judge built a fine residence, and the boys a fine business house, which was used for a saloon.

They helped to pay for the town site and expenses incurred and put improvements on their claims.

The old judge was both a doctor and a lawyer, and all four of the boys had been admitted to the bar, although Ed was the only one engaged in the business.

Ed Jennings[52]

Jennings & Jennings 1888.[53]

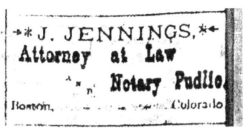

Although Konkel only recalls Ed Jennings practicing law in Boston,
it appears John also attempted a law practice in Boston per the ad above.[54]

Frank for a short time made good money in the locating business, Forney, afterward called Al, a short time in the saloon business, and all of them for a while in selling of town lots.

Frank Jennings[55]

But the money they made was lived up and drank up, and when in the midst of the seven years of famine spoken of in a separate article, they, with the others were in sore straits, and finally brought up in Oklahoma with absolutely nothing.

We never learned what the judge did with his dwelling or the boys with their business building;[56] but all such buildings after the town had gone down and the town and country to the dogs, sold in the neighborhood of from $25 to $75, and we presume the buildings went that way.

A.G. Wilson was another sorry victim of that old days break up. He was the treasurer of the town company, brought $3,000 with him, and the same amount in the bank at Winfield, Kansas.

Wilson was quiet in his ways, temperate, upright and honest in every way capable and a good manager.

He built a fine house and two or three business houses, helped to build and was a director in the $6,000[57] Boston hotel and put money here and there and elsewhere where he thought it would bring return, drawing the $3,000 he had left in the Winfield bank for these other purposes.

After three years of this kind of bookkeeping, Wilson found himself up against the fact that he didn t have enough money to take his family out of the country. He consequently had to borrow money from friends back east to get away.

He migrated to Wisconsin, went into the bee business and in few years had cleared up something like $10,000.

We believe he is now living a short distance out from Denver and that he is still in the bee business.

Fortunes again next week[58]

Fortunes Continued

Under the head of fortunes brought, made and lost Dr. Brown is noticeable rather for what he made and didn t lose, rather than for what he brought and lost. It is probable that $3,000 would cover what he brought with him, and even that may be $2,000 too high.

He first started a little one-horse dry goods store, with prices corresponding to the altitude of the country. Then he went into a 25x50 building, filled it with general merchandise, drugs and a compound closely allied to whiskey; and notwithstanding that the prices were lowered upward strictly in accordance with stand-pat principles, Doc Brown was the principal merchant in Boston up to the time he was hauled out of town under a load of fodder.

Doc Brown store ad 1888.[59]

For three years he did a big business and made a whole lot of money. Doc wasn t one of those who talks about his business, but himself and a clerk were kept on the jump waiting on customers from twelve to fourteen hours a day seven days a week and in three years it is likely he made some money - probably was worth at this time $10,000 to $15,000.

After making his final escape from town, never to come back again, the remaining goods were turned over to his clerk at probably a considerable amount below cost, which was a small loss compared to what he had made.

We haven t heard from or of Doc for 15 years, but at that time he was running a drug store in Missouri and was reported to be worth anywhere from $25,000 to $50,000.

The report of what he was worth at that time may have been exaggerated, but you could set Doc down in the heart of Africa with a bolt of calico, a case of pills and a recipe for white mule and at the end of the season he'd come out of with his colors flying and his clothes lined with money.

Tom Hambric was another sorry victim of those old days. Tom bought several town lots, built a 25x40 business building, built a fine residence and put in $2,000 or $3,000 of hardware.

Hambric Hardware 1888.[60]

It was the stock of hardware that floored Hambric. He put in stock after Boston was mostly built and after Boston was built there was very little more building done in the county.

Tom was a fine fellow and had a fine family. We never learned what he did with the stock of hardware, but he got out of the country with nothing, and we understand that for years he was in very strained circumstances having a hard time to support his family.

The instances which we have cited of those who dropped their wads in the west and had to either actually or figuratively walk out of the country and begin life all over again, are a few among the thousands, tens of thousands and even hundreds of thousands over the whole dry west who did the same thing.

Facts are, the settlement and deep population of the entire highland west was a tragedy in the temporal affairs of those well-meaning peoples. They came with buoyant hopes and high spirits, bringing with them their little all, with their families, and in the morning they found their little all gone, and a hungry wolf glowering in the doorway.

In Baca County, nineteen-twentieths of the settlers got up and drove away, or walked away, from their new homes-- downcast, dispirited, and many of them hopeless.

As it was in Baca County, so it was in the zone averaging probably 200 miles in width facing the whole east slope of the Rocky Mountains--homes left to the ruins, and towns afterward crumbling away until only piles of stone and holes in the ground were left to tell the story.

Why these good people fell down in this country-- that we now know they could have made good in, we told in an article serving as a prelude to these write-ups; and to put it in a few words it was the want of knowledge of dry country affairs and the need of dry country plants, and partly for the want of such plants-- which were afterward supplied and are now so much enjoyed.

While speaking here of those old-timers who dropped their wads and pulled their freight, we believe it is a good time to announce that in closing these articles-- in the indefinite future, we shall individually notice those old fellows who stayed with the country, struggled for some years with that frothing wolf at the door, finally kicked him into kingdom come, stood on their feet, begin to feel their oats, got chuck full of vinegar, took on their aristocratic airs, liking unto the psalmist Robinson Crusoe, who went up and down the land declaring— "I am the monarch of all I survey, my right there is none to dispute."

Next week will be something else. Watch for it[61].

Chapter 7: Doctors and Lawyers

"Half the cases of so-called heart diseases are only indigestion, and more men are scared to death than die any other way. How much? Three dollars please, and it is your own fault if you pay another doctors fee in the next ten years. Good day."

-The *Great Bend Weekly Tribune*, 1887

There were many ways to die on the Southeast Colorado frontier in the 1880s. Doctors were in high demand. Promotors for town companies often recruited doctors to their new town. They wanted to build towns which would entice more people to come and knew people wanted a full complement of businesses and services.

At least five physicians came to Boston in 1886 and 1887. Physicians could make much more money in the cities than in the country, so why would they hang their shingles out West? The dream of getting free government land contributed to the wealth of doctors Boston attracted as those who came were filing for homesteads just like everyone else. They wanted free land in the west.

Many advances in medical knowledge and technology occurred in the late 1800s including the germ theory of disease and the use of anesthesia during surgery. However, on the frontier, the space available in their bag or saddlebags limited the services doctors provided.

Doctors in Southeast Colorado, like most places on the frontier, serviced a large geographic area and were expected to treat everything from fevers and toothaches to stomach aches and sick livestock. Because there was little access to advanced treatment, whiskey often served as a quick and efficient painkiller. Sam Konkel indicates there was little sickness in Boston and even if there had been, there was not much money with which those who were sick could pay for services.

Doctors and Lawyers

After we are through with the lawyers and doctors that our good town was blessed with, we shall reel off a few odds and ends of little interesting somethings and nothings, related and disrelated, and then go after the final grand Boston round-up.

Following the grand round-up, will be a round-up of the old timers who stayed with the country and fought, bled and died for it; who actually and literally kept the home fires burning, and turned the dark clouds inside out -- when there was nothing but gloom in the land and the country seemed eternally doomed.

It has been a year the first prox. since these old time write-ups started, and it will probably be another year before they are brought to a final wind-up and maybe then some.

To get to these doctors and lawyers -- their quantity is probably of more interest than anything else particularly about them ⸗ unless it was the doggoned slim pickings by reason of their quantity and further reason of it's being slim pickings for everybody else.

There were five regularly licensed physicians in the town ⸗ more than there are at the present time[62] in Baca County.

Dr. Jennings

Of these we have already told a lot about Judge Jennings. Among other things mentioned is the fact that he held a doctor certificate, and that so far as we know was as good as any of the rest of them.

The old judge a few times expressed his regret that he was called "Judge Jennings" instead of "Doc Jennings" he undoubtedly thinking that the title had its weight in the matter of the practice or attainable business.

Dr. Jennings may have had a few cases, and may have assisted in a few cases, but not enough to say that he was practicing medicine. We would say that altogether he had less than half a dozen cases⸗ indeed considerable less, though as stated before, he was probably as good a doctor as any of them.

Dr. Brown

We have already told about Dr. Brown. So far as we know, he was a fairly good doctor, and we know he was occasionally called on as a doctor for his services.

In addition to a store, he kept a good supply of drugs and did a good part of the compounding for the country. We would say the rough guesses for actual practice made him less than $100 a year and it was consequently not worth fooling with.

Dr. McCrory

We are not sure where he came from but think from Arkansas originally, from Kansas directly.

He located a claim near Boston, but having nothing but his profession to hold him up, he at times-- all the time indeed, was sorely pressed for the wherewithal to meet the necessities of life, to say nothing about an occasional some-thing on the side that couldn t be classed as particularly essential. Doc stayed with the country until the last dog was hung, to use a slang expression and then went to we never learned where.

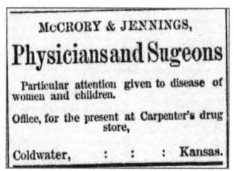

Jennings & McCrory worked together in Kansas
prior to moving to Boston.[63]

Dr. Milligan

Practically everybody in Baca County knows about Dr. Milligan. He being the one doctor out of the five of those old days who stayed with the country.

Because of the great number of doctors, because there was no money, and because he lived a little ways out of town, Dr. Milligan had no practice that brought him any money worth mentioning.

We shall have Dr. Milligan again when paying our special attention to those good old timers who refused to get out of the country, just because it wasn t a fit place for a white man to live.

Dr. Thomas Fletcher Milligan[64]

Dr. Hawk

We have mentioned Hawk before as one of the trustees of the town. He came to the town and we believe
stayed until the country went to pieces. Doc Hawk probably
enjoyed a larger practice than any of the others, but taking
what he actually collected wouldn t have been enough for
his own soul and body, to say nothing of other requirements.

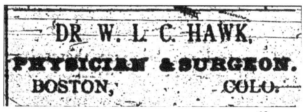

The above ad ran in the *Boston Banne*r in 1888[65]

Ditto Next Week[66]

The Lawyer Bunch

There were only four of them in the Jennings family ·
· the old man, John, Forney, and Ed. These boys had been
admitted to the bar, but none of them had any practicing
worth mentioning at the time and indeed nothing on the
paying basis until after their outlawry career in Oklahoma.
Ed was the only one of the boys that tried to do anything
at the business at Boston,[6] but we are doubting whether he

---

[6] It appears John ran a legal practice as he ran an ad in Konkel's paper March 8, 1888.

got as much as $50, or even $25 out of his law practice. All put together he and the old judge got about dirt.

Jerome Whitaker

Jerome made the fifth lawyer for Boston. He was a brother of Eugene Whitaker, ex-editor of the *Springfield- Herald* and ex-register of the Lamar land office, who s known by about everybody in Baca County.

Jerome was the city attorney of Boston, and presumably, for his services, he, like the town marshal was paid in script, which was worth just the paper it was printed on.

Jerome finally brought up in Washington, and we believe is now publishing some kind of trade journal.

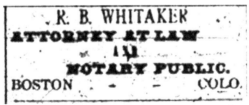

Whitaker ad in March 8, 1888 *Boston Banner*[67]

Col. Campbell

This was the one man whose title was handed down to him from official sources, he having been a lieutenant colonel in the Civil War.

Colonel Campbell didn t reside in Boston, but near enough for location purposes, he living four miles east. Campbell was the author of a law digest, relating mostly we believe to the common law as handed down by precedents. We never saw his book, and of course, wouldn t have known anything of the merits of the work if we had seen it; but the fact that he wrote a book on law which would stamp him as being well up in the profession.

The colonel wasn t much of a pleader. We never heard him in but one case, in which Judge Jennings had the other side. Campbell had the opening plea, and made a fairly lengthy talk; but when the old judge got through with him one was reminded of a pygmy and a giant.

We say we never heard him in but this one case. It is probable he never had any other case. Facts are that if the cases calling for a lawyer during the whole in that old time period had been divided up among the lawyers there wouldn t have been more than one or two apiece, and they of a petty nature.

Ordinarily it is supposed lawyers and doctors have a pretty soft soap in their respective lines of business, and ordinarily, under normal conditions, we suppose they feed pretty well and clothe accordingly; but the conditions at Old Boston and generally over the east end at that time were not normal.

There were only about three years of settlement, and after the first year, there was no money left in the country. During this time there was little sickness, and no money to pay for the little there was, while in law people were too busy to get in trouble, and after that they had no money to get them out.

The lawyers and doctors, as did the rest of the world, let their money get away from them during the first year, and then had to find some other way to live during the rest of their stay in the country.

Some Odds and Ends Next Week[68]

Captain John McCoach

Captain John McCoach was another of the Blackstone disciples of that good old town. We don t know as he ever got a doggoned cent out of the business. He tried to get a $25 fee out of Bill Thompson, who we will mention later, but it isn t very probable his efforts were successful.

The captain is noticeable here more for his indirect relation to the grand round up than for anything else in particular.

We don t know how he acquired his title. It might have been one of the myriads of cases where the title comes along and finds a man unappropriated and just settles down on him like a shade over a lamp or he might have bled and died for the title on the field of battle.

Captain McCoach came down from Vilas at the time of the five Vilas houses moving to Boston, only Cap didn t have anything to move except the possible extra suit of clothes-- and his title and profession, so far as we recall.

Vilas Hotel March 1887. Cap. McCoach is sitting far left on the porch playing cards[69]

He was a lawyer by profession, and so far as we now understood he knew his business as well as any of the rest of them; only people in those days were too busy guessing to do any litigating. Those that did litigate had very little money or not any at all, and so Cap McCoach was in this guessing school along with the thousands of others over this at that time doomed west.

Among Cap's clients was the Bill Thompson before mentioned, who in diverse ways became identified with the town s history.

Cap we believe had assisted Bill in the case growing out of the killing of Henry Savoy. Anyway, he had a fee against him of $25 for lawyer services, and hence when Bill came to town Cap stuck to him like a leach until Thompson returned to his headquarters in No Man s Land, where fees were not needed and litigations were not known.

We are guessing now that Cap McCoach never got his money out of Bill Thompson; but whether or not and nev-ertheless, we will have them both on the carpet at the general Roundup, and so will leave them for the present.

Something Else Next Time[70]

Chapter 8: A Few Personal Stories

"What are we to do about our band? So many of the old band have gone to Colorado that it appears to be impossible to keep up the old organization. Would it not be well to form an independent organization? Let all lovers of music agitate this matter, and then let a meeting be called to determine what line of action is for the best. The "brass horn tooters and the sheep-skin pounders" are necessary to our happiness, amusement and comfort. Let us keep up a good band."

-Ashland Weekly Journal, April 1887

The February 1887 issue of the Richfield, Kansas paper states,

"The Boston Town Company are men of capital with broad and liberal ideas. They believe in a policy of live and let live."[71]

The following pages summarize Konkel's recollections and include newspaper clippings which give us a more accurate picture of some of the less noticed and less notorious characters who came to southeast Colorado to settle in Boston in the late 1880s.

Bill Lindley and Geo. Nethercut

Bill was a man of some affairs, having accumulated some property, probably partly by labor, partly by business, partly by jockeying, and partly by gambling, and other tangible and intangible ways of getting money.

Bill was a big square built fellow and wanted it generally understood that he was or would be a bad man to monkey with, and that what he wanted he was able to get.

Bill and George made several trips to No Man's Land on their trading expeditions, and on one or two occasions represented themselves as U.S. Marshals, and by that means took some horses that probably the other fellow didn t have a very clear title to and got others by ways that were even more reprehensible.

This incident is mentioned here because it was some of these dubious ways of getting horses out of No Man's Land that was largely responsible for the final grand round-up of Boston, which we will reach later on these write-ups.

William H. Yaw

We are mentioning Yaw here because he was connected with a horse affair that really was the direct cause of the final Boston Grande round-up aforesaid, and which will be related when we get to that part of the story.

Yaw was none of the things that was mentioned in connection with Lindley and Nethercut. He was not a gambler, a jockey, a loafer, nor any of the other attributes that go into the dubious life of one of that nature.

When Yaw came to Boston about the spring of 1887, he built a livery barn and was counted an honest, industrious, upright man of affairs.

At one time, and maybe at other times, so far as we know, he went down into No Man's Land and brought back a number of horses, mentioned at the time it s quite an event, and nothing further was thought of the event until the day of the final roundup.

We here leave these three for the present but will have them all on the carpet at a later date.

Yaw brand notice from the March 8, 1888 *Western World*.[72] [73]

Thornburg

J. G. Thornburg, two miles northeast, has a well sixty feet deep, with five feet of water - *Boston World.*

Thornburg was the man who never knew that anyone else was talking, and it s because of that oddity that he s mentioned here. He had a grating, guttural voice, and the only thing he or anyone else could hear was that voice, it mattered not how many voices were in the battle.

We will mention two incidents as an illustration of this peculiar trait in the man's strange makeup.

The writer, besides being in the newspaper game, was in the loan business, and knowing that Thornburg was going to prove up, we drove out to his place to make him a loan.

As was always the case, he opens the (one-sided) conversation as we drove up, and he still had the floor something like an hour later when we finally drove away.

Did we make him the loan?

Forty times during that historic "conversation" we opened up our batteries on the loan proposition, and forty times Thornburg didn t hear anything but that deep grating guttural voice of his own.

"I hear you are going to prove up" "Do you want to borrow a dollar?" "Wait while -- I want to talk business." "I can loan you $1,000 on your place."

Nothing doing. The only thing we got out of that drive and the hour s effort were some watermelons the strange man loaded into our buggy while "we were talking."

Giving up all hopes of being able to be heard over that grating, guttural voice, we finally said "thank you for the melons," and drove away.

Another incident of the strange man the next time.[74]

A Few Personal Stories

Thornburg continued

The writer, Tom Hambric, Dr. Hawk, and Cap McCoach, were standing in front of the Hambrick Hardware store when Tom suddenly exclaimed:

"Here Comes Thornburg-- now when he comes up let s all go to talking at him at once and talk him down-- there mustn't be a smile cracked and no let up until he finds out we re talking."

As the man approached, that grating, guttural voice approached with him while his eyes were putting down a barrage a way to the rear of us.

As agreed, we all turned loose, talking directly to him or at him as fast as we could rattle and as hard as we could talk. We kept it up for what seemed to be five minutes, really probably not more than one minute, when one of the combatants burst out in a the big snort and guffaw, and of course the others followed suit.

Did he notice then?

Not on your tin type, as the slang expression goes. Those eyes just kept up their barrage firing a way to our rear and that falsetto voice kept right on grating and grinding without a break or a quiver; and on the impulse to move on he moved on with a kind of guttural grind and a grunt combined ⁓ and the entertainment was over for that time.

The Earth is Flat

One of the most familiar characters of Boston in those old days was a man by the name of Enock Swalley, interesting because of the powerful arguments he invariably led off on against the book information and teaching of the earth being round.

Everyone came to know Swalley, and many of them, some seriously and some earnestly, withstood and argued the case with him up one side and down the other.

Some of the powerful arguments of the man were ⁓ "the water would fall out of the ocean," "men and women when the earth turned over would be walking and standing on their head and, and they too would fall off." "Contrary to the Bible and God s teaching," etc. etc. etc.

One night we entered the grocery store when Swalley and "the boys" were having it up and down as to whether the earth was flat or round.

We listened for a while, and then one of the parties to the big log rolling wanted to get our editorial and reportorial understanding of things, they up and asked us if the earth were round or flat.

"Is the earth flat?" said we, "of course its flat⁓ just as it looks to be. This thing of things only appearing to be, primafaciedly absurd and won t stand the test."

"The sun, moon, and stars only appear to go around the earth, do they?"

"The next thing they ll be telling us is the clouds only appear to go around the earth, that the earth is really going around the clouds--just as reasonable."

"You might say people don t really walk-- they just appear to walk; -- it just appears to be that way."

"You might say nothing exists at all-- they just appear to exist-- inclusive of our dear selves."

That is the old know nothing information handed down from ancient times that would deny God the Bible, man and the devil.

It's easy enough to talk about things only appearing, but our sense of vision tells us better, the Bible, and all nature tell us better, and in the language of Abraham to the rich man in hell -- "if they believe not these, neither would they believe the one who rose from the dead."

And with this we ambled our way outward from the building and left the world cosmographers to wrestle with the mighty problem. Mr. Swalley, taking the floor to fur-ther expand the Bible doctrine in the case and to cinch the irrefutable arguments laid down of flatness versus roundness in the dimension of world affairs.

We never heard of Swalley after the breaking up of the country and the settlement, but we presume if he is living, he is still putting forth these powerful arguments in support of the primitive doctrine of the earth being flat, immobile, and the whole of the universe.

Next Week Again[75]

A Store Burglary

As we said on another occasion, there were times in the history of old Boston when a whole lot of people were guessing about the enigma of the soul in the body.

Anyway, one often wonders at any time how some people live, and about the fall and winter of 1888-89 these "some" in old Boston had a little more guess coming than is usual even with this "some" class.

And so it came to pass on that certain morning of a certain day in this dark period in the history of the west the news was megaphoned over town that Doc Brown s store had been burglarized the night before and numerous articles of value carried away inclusive of cigars, tobacco, jewelry, canned goods, etc., etc.

The persons who burglarized the store weren t giving out any information, and consequently just who the guilty ones were was a hard guess. Everybody including the bur-glars themselves, felt certain the guilty ones were within the city limits. But outside of the perpetrators that was about as near as the guess was to be made.

Now the facts are that it was only recently the writer himself learned the truth about that burglary, for which information we are indebted to the old time Boston veteran, ex-register Eugene M. Whitaker, now of Lamar.

We neglected to ask Mr. Whittaker how he got the information, principally because it wasn t really material; but the story runs as follows-- only names of the parties are emitted

According to the story four persons were implicated-- a certain doctor, a certain sometimes sign painter, and two gentlemen of leisure and clever in poker games.

The doctor s part in the game was to walk slowly up and down the street opposite the store, and to whistle a signal in case of danger. Two of the boys were inside gath- ering up contraband, while the third was on the outside receiving the stuff as it was handed out.

Something like $200 or $300 worth of stuff was pur- loined from the store, which didn t do Brown a great deal of harm. While at the present time we don t suppose the boys were any better off.[76]

Captain Parrott

J.B., J.B. Jr, and Robt. Parrott of Greensburg, Kansas have located claims 9 miles southeast and will soon have up their houses. J. B. is an old-time Kansan, having resided in that state over thirty years. He and sons expect to put in a store here – *Western World,* Apr 21, 1887

Captain Parrott came to be one of the most striking characters in the old town. He and his boys had no money, and the only thing the old captain himself ever "put in" was what he also got "around" in the way of firewater.

Left to Right: Al Jennings, Frank Jennings, Andy Capansky, Grandma Capansky, Abel Capansky, Bert Capansky, Ed Jennings, Grandpa Capansky, ??? Crockett and Cap Parrott at Capansky Saloon in Old Boston, 1888.

It wasn t very many days that his eyes weren t "bleard" with drink, and always when under the "fluence" he would let those he encountered know that he was a bad man-- a regular "holy terror."

The captain actually looked fierce, and with those eyes bleared he stood up in front of a rather timid person for the first time and exclaimed --

"I m a holy terror; I've a notion to whoop:" and then would tear lose with an ear-splitting "w-h-o-o-o-p," the timid one would tremble, and feel a great relief when out of harm s way.

"I'm a bad man;" "I m a holy terror; I have a notion to whoop," and then tearing lose with an ear splitting "w-h-o-o-o-p," was the captain s favorite way of enter-taining himself and everybody else when his eyes were bleary and his voice was husky; so after a time when the captain was so, some of the boys, some of the time, would beat him to it, and approaching the bad man would exclaim -- "I m a holy terror; I have a notion to whoop," -- "w-h-o-o-o-p," when the captain would look at them with a blank expression and pass on.

The captain was a surveyor and made some money in that way, but of course drank it up as fast as he made it.

That was thirty years ago, and as the old Captain was then probably sixty, we presume he many years ago passed over to where a bad man, holy terrors, and firewater are equally unknown.

Something else next time[77]

A Few Personal Stories

Jimmy Ward, Hero

Little Jimmy Ward is the hero of the hour, and now a great many of our boys want to go hunt desparados. It is a big thing, boys, unless you should happen to come out second best in the entertainment - **Western World**, Aug, 30, 1888.

On Monday afternoon Jimmy Ward, one of the posse after Billy the Kid and Chas. Hill, suddenly ran into one of the gang supposed to be Cock-Eyed Jones in the neutral strip, and after a few words both began firing. Cock-Eyed getting in first shot and instantly killing Ward s horse from under him. Ward jumped behind the horse and continued to shoot-- and had the last shot. All united in the hope and rather believe the fellow got enough lead in his carcass to hold him down. As a token of a skirmish, Jimmy brought in the fellas horse and a pair of mules he had that were stolen near Vilas, and a hole through his vest and coat. – *Western World* Aug 30 1888.

Little Jimmy was an unpretentious sort of fellow, and didn t have much to say about anything. He would have been the last man anyone would have thought of in the role of a hero.

Had he come back with a story without bringing back some evidence, as in the case of Columbus discovering Amer-ica, it would have been thought of only as an amusing story but there were the mules stolen near Vilas and there was a horse with a saddle up on him and about the least anyone can make out of it was that Jimmy had been to the front and in some kind of an engagement with the enemy.

Jimmie Ward was one of the Vilas bunch coming down with the five houses only about a month prior to the inci-dent-related.

At this time we do not recall whether he stayed there until the town went to pieces the next spring or not but he was never in any kind of business, and so far as we know was never heard of again after leaving the town in the country.

> On Monday afternoon J. Ward, one
> of the posse after Billy the Kid and
> Chas. Hill, suddenly run onto one of
> the gang, "Cock-Eyed Jones," and after
> a few words both began firing, "Cock-
> Eye" getting in fist shot, and instantly
> killing Ward's horse from under him.
> Ward jumped behind the horse and
> continued to shoot, and had the last
> shot. All unite in the hope and rather
> believe the fellow got enough lead in
> his old carcass to hold him down. As
> a token of his skirmish "Jimmy"
> brought in the fellow's horse and a
> pair of mules he had that were stolen
> near Vilas, and a hole through his vest
> and coat.—Boston World.

Little Jimmy Ward Story[78]

Freeman Newton and the Boston Band

These are all professional players. Many of them have
been teachers of band music for many years and are also
fine actors. It s intended to send this band eastwardly as
far as Washington during the coming fall and winter as
missionaries for our young city. The boys are mostly interested in Boston, and all have claims near town, and intend
to make this their home for all time to come - *Western
World,* July 25, 1887.

We are sorry to lose Freeman Newton from our midst.
He has an engagement as a musical director in the opera in
Topeka. Freeman besides being a skilled musician and com-
poser of music, is one of our most worthy and popular
young men – *Western World* Aug 2, 1888

The *World* took every opportunity to say something nice about the band, and the band boys in turn took every opportunity to let the editor know that they appreciated the nice things said about them.

The following are the members in order of the best band in the west:

Drum Major	Judge Jennings
E.b. clarinet	J. D. Newton
B.b. clarinet	Jacob Von Weber
E.b. Cornet	J. J. Jennings
B.b. clarinet	H. Holbrook
Solo Alto	Quincy Robertson
1st Alto	E. E. Jennings
2nd Alto	S. H. Parks
First BB tenor	E. H. White
2nd BB tenor	Melvin Hunter
Slide trombone	F. J. Newton
Bass horn	F. F. Jennings
E.b. Bass	A. J. Jennings
Bass drum	C. Edley
Snare drum	E. E. Easley

We open this talk particularly about Freeman Newton but a word about the other boys would be appropriate. The Jenningses were just natural musicians, and could handle the respective pieces with the skill of the very best. All four of the boys were in the band as well as the old judge himself.

When Forney and Frank were in the pen[7] -- different pens, they each belonged to the pen band, Frank, we believe acting as leader.

J. D. Newton, the elder of the Newton Boys was as good as either of the Jenningses. Mel Hunter, Ed White, and Quincy Robertson could easily have played in eastern bands, and all the others were good.

But Freeman Newton was the musical genius of the band, he not only playing anything with skill and perfection, but also composing much of the music the band played.

At the time of the quotation the band was at its best in both players and number of pieces but shortly afterwards the band begin to thin by reason of some going away.

We saw Freeman in Topeka about a year after he went there. The orchestra he was with was a fine one, but all looked to Freeman as the last word in musical technique, and often as did the Band at Boston, the orchestra would play Freeman s pieces not because they were Freeman s but because they were classy.

The June 8, 1922 *Garden City Herald* provides the following memory of the Boston Band playing for the celebration of Lamar, Colorado's first anniversary in 1887:

> *"Lamar celebrated her thirty-sixth birthday last week, and one of the events was the presence of a fleet of twenty five aeroplanes on their journey from Fort Sill, Oklahoma, to Denver. The best birthday celebration ever staged in that burg was probably the first one, when the town was one year old and had a population*

---

[7] Pen = Penitentiary. Both Al and Frank served time for robbing trains in Oklahoma.

of 1,500. Music was furnished by the Boston (Colorado) Silver Coronet Band. The Jennings brothers, of more or less questionable fame, were members of the band. Floats in the line of march dispensed free beer to the assembled multitude, which added considerably to the joy of the day. This is a feature of bygone days which not even the presence of an aeroplane can replace. "[79]

Another report recalls Free Newton leaving Boston,

> Free Newton is going to Topeka, Kansas, to live. He is offered a good salary for the use of his musical talent, and, as music is the passion and aspiration of his life, we cannot blame him for going. We are sincerely grieved, though, at the loss of little Free. He is a favorite with every one. Prosperity to you, friend.— Boston Banner. The same here, dear boy. We had thought that Richfield would secure you again, but, alas, fond hopes are shattered.

Freeman Newton is going to Topeka, Aug 1888[80]

We haven t seen or heard of the boy since but wherever he is he is no doubt the director of an orchestra or a brass band. That was thirty years ago so Freeman at this time would not be far from fifty five.

Next week again[81]

The Hambrics

The Hambrics were all good fellows, mild of manner and not meddlesome with other people s affairs, and consequently generally kept free of trouble.

There were four of them-- Tom the hardware merchant, Bob, Al, and George. Bob and Tom had families, the other two were single.

All the boys had claims, and we presumed were industrious; but none of them were equipped for farming, and as there was very little hiring, as we recall it now, the boys never had much to do.

It is because the boys were good fellows that we are here mentioning them, and will mention them to relate a few stories of them.

Bob was noted more than anything else for getting the wrong word at the wrong place at the wrong time. It took Judge Jennings to get over his strikingly ludicrous expressions, about all of which are now forgotten.

Boston Banner.

R. A. Hambrick has gone to Meade Center for the little woman. The Trinidad papers say some nice things of Bob as a commissioner, and they do him right. He is a good man for the place.

Ashland, Kansas news about Bob Hambrick[82]

Here is one though that has stayed with us and it will serve as an illustration. A horse had gotten in an old abandoned dugout cellar, and the boys were trying to get him out.

At this juncture Bob rode up, and after watching him for a while probably got the idea that they were worrying the horse, or that probably it was in vain anyway, or probably to show his horse wisdom exclaimed—

"O, Let him alone and he ll get out recently."

Bob was alone in these freakish expressions, but just because he would appreciate its telling and humor we will relate a rather humorous one on Al.

Al had gotten himself elected or appointed as a consta-ble, and so far as we know the case we are now relating is the only instance of his getting any money out of the office, and we don t know that they ever got any money even out of this case.

But Al felt the dignity of the position, and that was worth something to him. But the case was requiring an absent witness when the court instructed the constable to call the witness three times; and this the constable pro-ceeded to do as follows:

"John A. Wheeler – come to court, come to court, come to court."

There was a general all-around laugh at Al's expense, when the court instructed him to call the name three times. Al looked confused, but went to the door and tried it again this way –

"John A. Wheeler, John A. Wheeler, John A. Wheeler, come to court, come to court, come to court."

A Knife Play in Bachelor's Hall

This isn't exactly a change of subject, but turning on a particular incident.

George Hambric by some twist of the ego had gotten the idea he could face ol' Nick without flinching or batting an eye. He felt that he was so strong physically, morally and otherwise, that he could just walk up to a whole battalion of the James and Younger outfits and put them under arrest, and would do it if he had a warrant to serve on them.

This was George's theme; and he harped on the theme until people knew that he just couldn't be intimidated, and no highway outfit could make him throw up his hands. So after a certain incident it was the general comment that the boy had the conceit taken out of him anyway.

It was after Senor Boom had taken his departure to parts unknown and Senor Hard Times had taken possession of the land, for which reason some of the boys organized themselves into a bachelor's club in order to get down to the primitive cost of things in the struggle to keep soul and body together.

It was noon time, and a number of us standing out on the street talking, when suddenly there was a thump, thump thumpity thump in the bachelor's hall, as if some jackasses were trying the walls of the building.

Some of the boys on the outside threw the door open and jumped to one side, and after a time George backed out of the building, and a short time afterwards a fellow by the name of Gaul came out, the other bachelor-hall boys following.

George's right hand was badly cut – two or three ugly gashes on the inside, and it was bleeding profusely, while George himself was as white as a sheet.

Gaul meantime was standing on the sidewalk with knife in hand, ready for anything that might come up; and on Bob's making some remark about the cutting, Gual replied –"It isn't your put in, Bob – if you fellers want any more you can have it."

No one seemed to want any more, so George was taken up to the drug store and one of Boston's five doctors dressed his hand. As the dressing was progressing Gaul came in and said – "George, I'm very sorry. I'll pay the doctor and for the medicine – I'm sorry it happened."

What was it all about? Simply that George accused Gaul of having one more egg than the rest of them, and Gaul declared he didn't. That was all.

Something else next time.[83]

Squire Dalzell

About half the time he was called as above, and about the other half of the time was called Sam Dalzell; but that didn't make any difference, so long as they didn't call him too late for his chuck.

We are noticing Dalzell here not because he was a dog-goned good fellow, but because he was the best billyard player in all the west, and because of his very formal expression –

"Verily I say unto you these words,"

Because he is a reader of these old-time write-ups (on the side), and we consequently would not want to pass him unnoticed; and for other reasons, inclusive of goodwill and the hope of his continued future happiness.

One of Sam's most thoroughly understood accomplishments was his manipulation of the billyard cue. So far as we ever learned he never played any champion games, but in making the ivories do as he wanted them to it would have taken something of a champion to have laid it over him.

If there was anything that Sam liked better than a game of billyards, it was another game of billyards. If there was a stay in Boston that he didn't play from one game up, it was when he forgot to get up, which he never did, or he was off his feed, which we never knew him to be, or there were a whole lot of other things, which we never knew to happen. He wasn't a pool hall loafer, but several times during the day, and generally at nights, he would drop in for a game with someone, and if there wasn't anyone he would have a game with himself.

Of course, we presume Dalzell had a claim out some-where, but we really never knew him to live outside of the city limits as long as overnight -- so far as we now re-member. A preemption though only required a six months' residence, and counting, one might in a week, constitute residence, it is possible he may have proved up a preemption; or he may have had a claim and never proved it up, as did thousands of others in the west at that time.

We don't know the time when Dalzell wasn't a justice of the peace -- he seemed to bring that little protégé right here with him when he came and kept it under his wind and watchful care while in the country and hence was gen-erally known as Squire Dalzell.

Sam took special delight in mimicking the cute little ways of children, which he could do as Roosevelt would say to a frazzle, to the great amusement of the children themselves.

"Verily, I say unto you these words," was one of Dalzell's favorite and formal expressions when in a jocular conversation with grown-ups.

Hard up? Well, Squire never had any millions to pay his hotel bills and to buy fine raiment with, that's certain. Facts are, like everybody else at and around old Boston, and the whole west, so far as that is concerned. Sam entered by way of the blowing of the horn, and of course, as he was going towards, or passing to and through the other end of it, there was a whole lot of the time that he was kept guessing.

Before leaving Dalzell, having spoken of his adeptness at and fondness of billyards, we want to say we don't think he ever did any gambling. Indeed, we don't know as he ever played cards at all.

Fifteen years after the country had broken up and Dalzell and everybody else was gone we heard of him at Arkansas City, Kans. and recently through Attorney Mail, we learn that he is in Denver, Mr. Mail stating that after reading the old time write ups himself he passes them on to our old Boston contemporary Daniel and that Daniel passes them on to Dalzell.

Squire, here's looking at you.
Something else next week.[84]

Strange Resemblance

Talk about your doubles! We will relate an incident of resemblance that we never before ran across and have never ran across since.

Down at old Boston, there was a man by the name of Barney Wright whom we will notice immediately after the close of this sketch.

Barney was a strong, heavy, square-built man, rugged with very distinguishable features and piercing black eyes.

Now for the strangeness of the resemblances. One day we were walking down the street of Old Granada when suddenly we met Barney Wright. We stopped impulsively and wondered why he didn t recognize us, and almost felt that it was a breach of acquaintanceship not to speak to him and the men.

Just about a mud-colored negro - we would say forth blood, though probably half.

There was the same square build, ragged features, shaggy eyebrows, piercing black eyes, the same countenance, the same walk- everything the same only he was probably a quadroon negro instead of a white man.

Barney Wright

The incident of the resemblance brings us to an incident in the life of the man himself. Barney was a spectacular trader and gambler; that is, he played cards for money, though not making it a profession. It was Vilas, about the summer of 1888 and Barney Wright and some Vilasites were in a game of cards.

It was probably 2 or 3 a.m., when revolver shots rang out in the air, just how many nobody knew, and just who shot them nobody would tell

Next Week Again[85]

A Few Personal Stories

Barney Wright Continued

One of the shots fired found the left side of Barney Wright and lodged somewhere near the spine.

It was "officially" announced that the shot that caught Barney came in through the window, but a number of shots were fired, and probably Barney himself didn t know just who it was who nipped him.

Incidentally, after the shooting, he was moved to the hotel, and the next morning was brought to his home in Boston.

Doctors Brown and Hawk were the doctors having charge and for something like three weeks did all they could in their power for the patient, but finally after great hopes, blood poisoning set in, and a few days thereafter Barney passed away to the great unknown, where firearms and booze are equally outlawed, and the card playing and crap shooting will be no more.

We are not certain, but presume Barney was laid to rest in the Boston cemetery, and his remains could now be found in an unmarked grave in that old time morgue.[86]

W. B. Wright marshal of Boston, Colo., was shot at Vilas on Saturday morning last at 2 o'clock. Particulars are meagre. The wounded man, it is thought, will die, having been shot with a 45-revolver, the ball penetrating side of hip, striking bone, and its range being undetermined. The statement is made that Wright was probably shot with his own revolver after having given it up. Some other particulars equally indefinite have been mentioned. The sum of the information, however, is that one victim has been shot down as the result of a feud between rival towns.

Barney Wright was serving as Boston Marshal at the time of the shooting.[87]

Bob Crossman

Our readers will remember that we had Bob Crossman on the carpet at the early stage of these write-ups; but as we have a good many new subscribers since then, we will state briefly that Bob was the editor of the Vilas Democrat, was one of the promoters of that town, was somewhat of a lawyer, and was one of the last to give it up when the county seat went to Springfield and the country went to pieces.

Bob always had a penchant for wanting to run things, and because of his often going out of his way to humor this particular inclination he very often found himself in trouble and often in pretty deep water. [88]

Crossman, the ragged (jack)assed ex-preacher, ex-blatent republican, ex demo-crat hater, fawning hypocrite; leering demagogue, kicked-out postmaster and tin-horn gambler, indicated a desire in this week's Vilas Democrat to further steep his slum-scented fingers in the filth of a cesspool of spattering word bosh. Go to it, wheybelly! Get there, cockeye. —Boston Banner. This is a sample of the slashes the Vilas and Boston papers are throwing at each other for the present. "Let 'er go Gallagher," boys. It is amusing to stand off at this distance and look on. We had the same experience a few short months ago ourselves.

Here is a sample of Bob Crossman's writing eliciting a response from *Boston Banner* editor George Daniels. It seems from this and other reports he probably was pretty good at getting himself into "pretty deep water". [89]

The following shows Crossman mixing it up in Coldwater, Kansas with none other than John Jennings in a time prior to coming to Colorado as well as providing another example of how the "Jenningses" were willing to take steps to fix a "problem" when someone got in the way of their objectives:[90]

Monday afternoon about 1 P. M the cry of fight brought a croud to the street, and it was found that two men were fighting near the postoffice. Young John Jennings was punishing R. A. Crossman for the attack which the latter made in last weeks *Republican* on Probate Judge Dr. Jennings, the father of the assailant. Crossman's nose was some what damaged, and his face and head showed some scars. Jennings was, so far as could be seen, unhurt. A warrant was sworn out for Jenningls arrest and put in Sheriff Bower's hands. The case was tried before Justice Hutchins, Jennings pleading guilty. The fine was put at three dollars, and the cost two dollars and twenty five cents. The crowd immediately made up the amount, and paid the cost and fine.

Chapter 9: The Neutral Strip

"Somebody asked ex-Governor McCook, who is an authority on all territorial land questions by virtue of his long residence in and familiarity with that part of the country, whether there was any government in "No Man's Land" –any execution of the law. Well, I should say there was, replied McCook. You go along the border of the neutral strip and you'll think so. Every few miles there is a post with a notice like this: 'Any ___of a ___ coming on this ranch will get his scalp taken.' Oh yes there's plenty of government on the strip, and you don't have to travel far to run against it."

-The Topeka Capital, September 1885

In 1880, the cattle business of the far west, which for 10 years had been smoldering with a pale uncertain glow, burst into flames. In these golden days of the open range cattle boom, No Man's Land, the Neutral Strip or The Strip was an imperial stock growing country. The place with multiple names is now referred to as the Panhandle of Oklahoma. Lacking enacted laws, this geographical waif, one hundred and seventy miles east and west, by thirty five north and south was especially in the western end well sheltered, abundantly grassed, and watered by frequent perennial streams.

The story of the Neutral Strip begins when Texas sought to enter the Union in 1845 as a slave state. Federal law in the United States, based on the Missouri Compromise, prohibited slavery north of 36°30' parallel north. Under the Compromise of 1850, Texas surrendered its lands north of 36°30' latitude, which became the south border of "The Neutral Strip." This created a 35 mile wide and 170 mile long strip of land with no state or territorial ownership. This land was officially called the "Public Land Strip." This area remained without legal jurisdiction from 1850 until 1890.

The Compromise of 1850 also established the eastern boundary of New Mexico Territory at the 103rd meridian, thus setting the western boundary of the strip. The Kansas-Nebraska Act of 1854 set the southern border of Kansas Territory as the 37th parallel. This became the northern boundary of No Man's Land. When Kansas joined the Union in 1861, the western part of Kansas Territory was assigned to Colorado Territory, but did not change the boundary.[91] In 1886, the Neutral Strip's westernmost section was located just below Las Animas County, Colorado. Fifteen miles north of the Neutral Strip's north border, Boston became the second of seventeen towns to be started in the next two years on the windswept Colorado prairie.

The Boston Colorado founders brought hopes of becoming the county seat of a new county and soon would spar for the title with multiple towns having similar dreams.

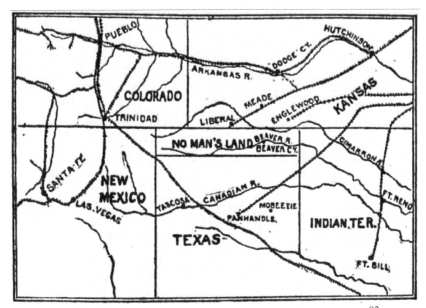

Map of the Neutral Strip, also know as No Man's Land or The Strip[92]

To understand the role of the Neutral Strip in the history of Boston we will begin with the legend of Robbers Roost located just north of present day Kenton, Oklahoma. The most famous occupants of the Roost in the years prior to the Boston era were the Coe Gang lead by the notorious William Coe. Numbering between thirty and fifty members, the gang began forays to Fort Union, New Mexico, and Fort Lyon, Colorado, to steal army horses and mules in the late 1860s.

The hideout was reputed to provide its occupants entertainment with a full-sized bar, piano, and a plethora of girls. Although the Coe Gang's time ended in the late 1860s it continued to be a haven for those of less than pristine character.

Ed Maxwell, one of the regulators involved in the final days of Boston, lived at Robbers Roost. The cow boys and many others in this story spent quite a bit of time going back and forth between Boston and the Neutral Strip. The livery stable man, Yaw, also conducted business in the Neutral Strip.

From 1850-1890 it had no official government at all. Understanding this lack of "official governance" provides insight on why Boston was greatly influenced by a lawless element.

Boston's town president, Albert Hughes, was also down in the Neutral Strip exploring property in 1885, nearly a full year, prior to coming to Colorado. An 1885 issue of the Ashland (Kansas) Clipper provides us the following,

> *"A party consisting of John W. Ayers, C. O. Taylor and son of Winfield, A. Hughes, W.F. Beach and King Berry, started yesterday on a hunting and prospecting tour down through No Man's Land."*[93]

The 1880s were a time when this area was controlled mostly by outlaws, cattle barons, and foreign-owned companies such as the Prairie Cattle Company. It is an area which has always intrigued and confounded people, a home to brave pioneers and outlaws alike.

In 1889 a *New York Sun* Reporter ventured into the Neutral Strip and provided the following description.

NO MAN'S LAND.

A Sun Reporter's History of a Strange Country.

BEYOND UNITED STATES LAW.

Counterfeit Money Made Without Hindrance.

A REFUGE FOR CRIMINALS,

But, on the Whole, an Orderly Frontier Community.

The Peace Preserved with Rifles and Six-shooters.

Header to Sun Reporter's 1889
Report on the Neutral Strip.[94]

The descriptors above are indicative of the influence of "The Strip" on Boston. In addition to "The Strip's" reputation for lawlessness, there was general lack of understanding about exactly where it was. One of the many examples of this confusion is encompassed in the Tuesday, August 30, 1881, issue of The *Dallas Daily Herald* which proclaimed,

> *"By some awkward oversight a tract of land embracing 2,800 square miles of public domain belongs to no state or organized territory. It lies north of the Panhandle of Texas, is one hundred and sixty miles long and thirty miles wide and is bounded north by Kansas and Colorado, east by Indian Territory, south by Texas and west by New Mexico. It is marked "public land" on the land office maps, but how it escaped government survey is a mystery. A survey of it has just been ordered. The tract of land referred to what is known as Greer County in this state has tacitly been given by congress. We say tacitly because there has been no act giving it to Texas."[95]*

A Wednesday, August 31, 1881, letter to the editor of the *Dallas Daily Herald* in response to the previous story quickly corrects the articles description of the Neutral Strip as what was then known as Greer County Texas.

> *In Tuesday's issue, an explanation of the existence of a strip of land between the panhandle of Texas and Kansas, which is included in no state or territory, you fall into a radical error in supposing it to refer to Greer county, Texas. Greer county, while on some maps shown to be a part of the leased Indian territory*

on the east, (embracing "Fort Sill and sundry" reservations whereon the wild tribes are located) is as truly a part of Texas as treaty language, with maps attached, can establish a fact -- boundary established by the United States and Spain in 1819 and ratified by Mexico in 1831.

But this strip of public land stands on an entirely different basis, just as any other unorganized territory of the United States would stand, and as all the lands now in Kansas, Nebraska, Wyoming etc., before their erection into territorial existence.

There are also many references which have confused this place thinking it was Indian Territory. The common theme is the Neutral Strip or No Man's Land was a place no governing body knew what to do with for 40 years.

The canyon hideouts of the Neutral Strip are also frequently mentioned in newspapers of the time, and it often had something to do with horse thieves. Boston was often mentioned in association with horse thieves and subsequently with the Neutral Strip as the following news reports attests.

Bold Horse Thieves.

A Richfield, Kansas news report tells the story of A. C. Bridges, Cal Hait and Charles Perkins. They went to Colorado to an area on the border of Colorado and the Neutral Strip after wild plums. They took with them two wagons, two mule teams and one extra horse. While camping in the Neutral Strip thirty five miles southwest of Boston, they hobbled the animals and turned them loose to graze. After eating supper they started to look up the teams, but arrived on the scene in time to see two men driving them off, the whole five, stealing them before their eyes in broad daylight. The party arrived home today. One mule team was as fine as any in southwest Kansas. Thompson Kid[96] is reported to have held up a traveler and taken his horse from him, on Bear creek Saturday. Colorado is worse than the strip for lawlessness of this kind.[97]

The report above shows the direct connection between Boston and the Neutral Strip family mentioned.[98]

NO MAN'S LAND.

Scenes Among the Bandits and Horse-Thieves of that Section.

A gentleman named J. Barnes, residing in Missouri, arrived in this city last evening, direct from the western part of No Man's Land. He went down there nearly a week ago in search of a younger brother, who, he had reason to believe, had been induced to join the outlaws of the strip. He was not disposed to talk much about what he saw, but after repeated questions in regard to the condition of things, he said that he had found a bad lot of men, but when he told them his business and they became satisfied he was telling the truth, he was allowed to make a search for his brother. He paid liberally for services rendered and secured an escort to the different camps. He says that there are three camps in Squaw canyon and that he thinks there are nearly 250 men in all the camps. They had plenty of horses, enough to mount every man in the gang. Mr. Barnes said that among the horses he noticed quite a number of superior animals, and he thought that they were much better than you generally find in the west, showing that they had been well selected. The outlaws were not disposed to talk much about their affairs, but were very anxious to get hold of information as to the action of congress in regard to the strip. The men he saw were for the most part quite young and some of them mere boys. A large majority of them were men of intelligence and presented the appearance of being determined characters. He thought they did not present the appearance of being cut-throats, but it was his opinion they would fight to the death. He was asked if he could tell what these men intended to do in the near future. In reply he said he only knew what he saw; they had told him nothing as to their intentions. He did not think they would make anything by remaining in camp. He did not know what they did with their horses or what market they found for them. Mr. Barnes left for his home on a night train.

Another connection to the Neutral Strip,
a common destination for horse thieves who frequented Boston.[99]

Chapter 10: Not That Billy the Kid

"Colorado offers opportunities for both rich and poor. It is a good country for poor men who have health, industry and intelligence, as well as for men with capital. It is a bad country for fools and rascals, although rascals do sometimes flourish temporarily. We don't want any more of them."

-Bent County Register, 1887

Although they may not have wanted any more "rascals" in southeast Colorado they got their fair share. One of the biggest rascals shared a moniker with one of the more famous characters of the old west. When people hear "Billy the Kid," they think of Henry McCarty; also known as William H. Bonney. Bonney was an American wild west gunfighter who took part in New Mexico's Lincoln County War. In pre-Baca County Colorado, there was another young man of questionable character known as "Billy the Kid." Although news reports of the day sometimes confused the two, it wasn't the more famous "Billy the Kid" we are speaking of from this point forward. To be clear, Boston's Billy the Kid was William Smith aka William Cornelius or Billy Cornelius. He was said to be a convicted horse thief before becoming the city marshall of Boston at age 16.

Alberta Clark, daughter of Boston restaurant owner J.J. Burnett, says of Billy,

"There used to be a horse wrangler working for the ZH that was nick-named Billy the Kid. He was pretty tough and dressed to look the part. He'd come into town with two big six-guns and cartridges and swagger around. The town folks got the idea that he'd make a swell marshall, so they put him in. He got well acquainted with the door locks—all the old-fashioned drawbar kind. He'd cut a hole in one and slip the bar and help himself to anything he wanted, always forgetting, somehow to leave money. One time he got a full suit of clothes out of Doc Brown's store (this was before the fight that ended Old Boston) one night, came and pried a board off our chicken coop, went in and changed his clothes and then went on his way rejoicing. In addition to stealing store things he stole cattle and horses as well"[100]

Other reports indicate until May 1888, Billy the Kid had been town Marshal of Boston, Colorado. When a U.S. Marshal showed up to arrest him on an old charge, he suddenly left. The town knew about this charge but disregarded it because it had happened in his teenage years. This is consistent with various reports of Cornelius.[101]

There were many reports of Billy's illegal activities in the area. According to the (Richfield) *Leader Democrat*, he gave the name of William Cornelius but his real name was Smith. "His mother is living near Caldwell, Kansas, and from her the day before he left he received $200, the result of her summer's farm produce. He wrote for the money to pay his debts." (*Leader Democrat* quoting the *Boston World*).[102]

He joined up with the Neutral Strip horse thieves and apparently talked them into revenge on Morton County Kansas. They sent some prostitutes to case the town, but they were arrested and fined. The suspicious characters with them cleared out also.

Then someone set fire to the Blue Front Livery in Richfield. It was suspected this was a distraction to commit robberies while everyone was busy with the fire. The fire was detected early and nothing happened. Next "Billy The Kid" showed up at nearby Taloga. The banker noticed him hanging around, set the timelock on the vault, and left. "Billy" held a woman customer hostage and got a few dollars from a storekeeper before leaving.[103]

Apparently, the gang had been causing as much trouble for Boston and Minneapolis, Colorado as well because they got up a posse of 150 men which chased them into the corner of Kansas where a Richfield posse joined them and shortly was also joined by a group from what would be the present day Boise City, Oklahoma area.[104]

> THE capture of Wm. Cornelius (alias, "Billy The Kid") by a couple of farmers near Boston, Colo., has greatly alleviated the fears felt by settlers against outlaws of No-Man's-Land. Perhaps never in the history of crime has there been so much deviltry committed by one so young and in so short a time. Horse stealings by the score. Bank and highway robberies were his speciality. He is eighteen years old and was at one time Marshall of Boston, Colorado.

The *Coffeville Weekly Journal* report above generically states Billy's capture was by a couple of farmers, only a slight difference from from Konkel's version.[105] Even John Jennings got in on the chase for "Billy the Kid" into the Neutral Strip in 1888.

> *"A week ago John Jennings and others left Boston, Colorado in pursuit of horse thieves. In the Neutral Strip the detachment overtook Billy Cornelius, an ex marshal of Boston, and one companion, both of them horsethieves, drying their clothing after a rain. The two leaped upon horses bareback and escaped. Some stolen horses and arms were captured. Part of the detachment returned with these while the rest of the detachment followed the thieves. The pursuing party reinforced*

by cowboys from about the Z.H. ranch it is believed, were guided
by the flight of Cornelius and his companion to the principal
rendezvous of the terrible band of thieves who are a scourge to
Southeastern Colorado. It is believed that the reported battle has
resulted in the total destruction to the main camp of outlaws
though. Here and at Folsom and Clayton this evening there was
no particulars only a meagre report of a pitched battle. "[106]

BAD CITIZEN CAPTURED.

Numerous reports document the capture of the Kid. Billy was
captured six miles from Boston and was taken to Granada, Colorado
where Deputy Sheriff Mott, of Boston and other officers took the train
for Trinidad. The papers, included the *Leadville Evening Chronicle*
in Sept of 1888, reported he was chased by thirty-two men from
Boston and Stonington. Their report says,

"This party was well mounted and armed and they went to
the house of Billy's uncle who lives near Springfield, on a Friday
night. Eight miles from Springfield they ran on him at half-past
10 o'clock at night. It was moonlight, and he could be plainly
seen and recognized. The party opened fire, but Billy leaned

over in his saddle and put spurs to his horse, which was a good one, and soon outdistanced the party, though they fired fully two hundred shots at him. He had a pair of good ponies which he was leading, and these he let go as soon as the firing commenced. They were captured and proved to be the pair which he had stolen in the neighborhood. Nothing more was seen or heard of him until Sunday night. A farmer was passing a claim house he knew to be vacant, and seeing a light, he looked into the building and recognized the Kid, who was cooking his supper. He covered the gentleman with a double barreled shotgun and called to him to throw up his hands. This Billy lost no time in doing. The farmer intended to take him to Boston, but the Kid begged hard not to be taken there, as he said the people of Boston would hang him. The farmer was at least prevailed upon to take him to Granada, where he turned him over to the officer. He said to an aquaintence on the depot platform in this city this morning:
"Good-bye. I will be back again in about five years. *"*[107]

The farmer, according to Sam Konkel, is Frank Lepel who along with his brother ran a blacksmith and carriage shop in Boston. In additon, Lepel was deputy to Billy when the Kid was Boston's marshal.[108]

Frank Lepel and his brother were Blacksmiths in Old Boston.
Although the quality of this ad is poor I wanted to include as the Lepels are one of the
few family names from Boston which made it to the modern era. [109]

One difference between Konkel's version and the version the news reported about the chase of Billy by the posse is that Konkel says he was visiting his mom and stepfather while the news report indicates he was visiting an uncle near Springfield. Konkel writes of Billy as follows,

Billy the Kid

Billy might have dropped down from the clouds, so far as anything was known of his coming. But he didn't. Instead, he came up out of No Man's Land[110], and like other notorieties from that part of the world was known as a cow boy.

About this time it came to be a kind of policy of Boston to pay special honor to those so-called cow boys, and Billy became consequently a kind of stepbrother to the town.

For many moons Billy came and went -- would be in Boston a short or long time, and then would be absent a short or long time.

During this time we don't presume that he had very much money with him and probably very often not any; and where he got what he did have, Boston neither knew or stopped to care about.

In the course of time, the town was duly incorporated; Billy then having become one of the fixtures of the town, was officially made the marshal of Boston.

We are not sure of the remuneration, but believe it was $30.00 per month. However, as it turned out it was immaterial whether it was $30.00 or $100.00 as the pay was in script, which proved in the end to be the same thing as so many blank pieces of paper.

As marshal, Billy did as well as anyone, and in some cases apparently displayed a fearlessness in making certain arrests that made him a subject of admiration.

Probably scores of times Billy disarmed the drunken desperado Newt Bradley, whom we mention in a separate article, and some other cow boys also.

For a long time after being appointed as marshal, Billy stayed with his knitting; but gradually he began to drop out of town and then back again ⁓ as in the first place probably partly caused by his nature, and partly by the depreciation to the entire worthlessness of the script with which he was paid for his services.

In the course of time we believe after his becoming marshal, Boston got the information that for some youthful indiscretion, Billy the Kid had served an apprenticeship in a reform school. However, that having been some depredation of his minor days, it was passed over as having been lived down.

Farther along in the course of time, an occasional horse came up missing, and still further along it became known that Billy had gone into the business.

It came about in this way: Billy had a girl a couple of hours ride out of town, and one day one of the missing horses was found at her place. Upon being questioned, the girl said Billy had made her a present of the horse.

The girl herself was innocent on the matter. The horse at that time wasn't worth over $10.00 or $50.00 and Billy explained to her that he was going away and hence wanted to give the horse to her.

A posse was at once organized to hunt for the said Billy. For weeks and weeks they would hear that he was here and then there, but always when the posse got there he was somewhere else.

Billy's mother and stepfather lived out on the edge of the cedars and one-day positive information was received that Billy was there and that a posse getting there that night could get him.[111]

Accordingly, a mounted posse of twenty men about midnight rode up to the house and called. The posse apparently being short of generalship and war tactics, the first thing they knew Billy was mounting his horse a short distance from the house, and the horse s feet were clattering on the turf.

As soon as the discovery was made, twenty bullets whizzed through the air in Billy s direction, but Billy and his horse were both unharmed, and the posse came back home, feeling chagrined at the way they had mummixed things up.

Once more it came to pass that Billy was here and there, and then there and here and then here and there. Often he would stay in some dugout when the occupant was temporarily away, and invariably on such occasions would cook his meals, sit down and read and smoke, sleep comfortably in the fellow's bed and then in the morning leave a note thanking the host for his kindness, and ride away before the day had broken,

Billy again next week[112]

Billy the Kid Continued

We will digress here long enough to relate an embarrassing position of a certain one of the city trustees (the mayor) in connection with Billy's reappointment as city marshal.

For some reason, Billy the Kid had gotten in bad with the Jenningses, and the old judge was bending heaven and earth to lay the boy on the shelf.

Dr. Hawk was the mayor, and was in sympathy with Billy, but naturally didn't want to antagonize the Jennings outfit. He was in hopes he wouldn't need to vote at all.

The vote was by ballot, and when the ballots were counted there were an even number for Billy and the other feller, and all the Jennings eyes at once turned to Hawk.

Just a moment the doctor hesitated, then hastily he wrote a name on a slip of paper, and dropping it in the receptacle exclaimed – "Billy the Kid"

Judge Jennings snorted his displeasure, and the meeting adjourned. Billy had no intentions of continuing as marshal of the town.

What he wanted from the first was to prevent the Jenningses from kicking him out, and when he had succeeded in that he quietly handed in his resignation; and we believe that ended the marshal business in Boston.

So far as was ever learned Billy had no connection with anyone else, either at Boston or the neutral strip, in his outlaw transactions. We think it likely, however, that he had co-workers in the strip, and that he would discover the horses and capture them, and then turn them over to the other fellows to dispose of.

It was probably three months after Billy dodged the posse and the bullets in the cedars that Frank Lepel, Billy's one time deputy thought he would take a night off from Boston to visit his farm four miles west of the town, thus to live up to the habitation requirements of holding down government land.

Whether because of knowledge of Billy's penchant of aiding settlers in holding down these claims, by his presence there when they were away or for some other cause, Lepel on this occasion had some kind of gun with him -- shotgun or repeater.

On approaching his occasional home, Lepel made the discovery that he had company, as a bright light was shining through the window in his direction.

Approaching the house (half dugout) Indian file, he peered in through the one-sash window, and discovered that his uninvited guest was the notorious and much wanted desperado, Billy the Kid – cow boy and one-time marshal of Boston.

Billy was sitting with his feet cocked up on the table, smoking a cigarette, and reading what might have been a love letter from his best girl.

Without arousing the reckless horsethief from his occupation, Lepel as we are now supposing, got a resting bead on the lad, and then advised him of the fact and that if he made any false moves the county would be shy one horsethief the next second.

We are also supposing that he ordered the reckless one to face the other way, take the gun out of its holster and lay it on the table, then to take the ugly weapon by its muzzle and advance with the other hand extended skyward.

That then with both hands extended, the one holding the muzzle of the gun, he loosed the latch strings of the window, turned it on its hinges, laid the gun outside. Then with one hand still skyward, he opened the door, stepped back into the room (with both hands skyward), and stood attention till the host had time to circulate inward by the doorway.

Anyway, said Lepel captured his bold and daring visitor, and upon said Billy's special request brought him to town and turned him over to constable Johnnie Mott, who also on Billy's special request, started with him at once for Lamar, thence to be taken to Trinidad and be turned over to the sheriff.

The reason of Billy's anxiety in the matter was that he feared the consequences of tarrying in Boston, as the town was pretty well worked up over his depredations, and Judge Lynch was presumably "rarin to go."

While Billy was awaiting his trial in Trinidad, the writer visited him in the county bastille.

"Billy," said we, "this didn't pay you -- a crooked life never pays anybody."

"But what was I to do?" asked Billy; "I tried to be honest and served old Boston well, but they paid me scraps of paper that I couldn't eat and nobody else would have."

"Yes, Billy, but its better to get down to work at a dollar a day, than it is to work for the state for nothing."

Well, Billy had his trial, at which half a dozen Bostonians appeared as a witness, and was given five years in the pen at hard labor.

We are presuming that he got out in about three years on good behavior, and think it likely that sometime after getting out he may have gone back to the old life, and that probably a third time he may have served a sentence in the pen.

However, so far as we have learned, nothing was ever heard of him again, and of course we have no information of whether he quit the old life or whether he didn't

Something else next week.[113]

A Few Odds and Ends

Thomas Fletcher Milligan and Charles Fletcher Milligan branding near Boston, CO.[114]

JJ Cowboys in Southeast Colorado. The JJ was part of the Prairie Cattle Company.[115]

TORNADO HACK LINE !

We the undersigned will run a Tri-Weekly Hack
Line between

BOSTON AND RICHFIELD

For the accommodation of Passengers, Express and Mail until Aug.
1st. After which it will be made a daily line. A good outfit and
always on time will be our motto.

COX & GUMM,
PROPRIETORS.

The Boston to Richfield Stage 1887.[116]

More JJ Cowboys in Southeast Colorado.[117]

First Anniversary of the City of Boston Colorado.

HEADQUARTERS INVITATION COMMITTEE ON BOSTON's FIRST ANNIVERSARY, Nov. 14, 1887.

To the Citizens of Syracuse, Kansas—Greeting:

The citizens of Boston and committee on invitation extend a cordial and hearty invitation to the citizens of Syracuse, Kansas, to attend in delegation the First Aniversary of the City of Boston, Colorado, on the 24th day of November, 1887.

The following speakers have been invited and will be present: Governor Adams, Sec. of State Rice, Hon. Wm. Sims, Hon. F. T. Arbuckle, Hon. F. H. Shrock, Gen. Wm. Henton, Sen. Beverrilla, Gen. Sopris, Judge Hines and others.

There will be a free barbecue, and balloon ascension, racing, orations, fireworks, grand supper and ball. Five hundred posters giving full programme have been distributed.

This is a special invitation to the citizens of Syracuse, for whom the people of Boston entertain the warmest friendship. We will expect one hundred people from your town.

A. HUGHES,
GEO. DANIELS,
ED. WHITE,   Com.
J. C. FISHER,
SAM KONKLE,

Boston's First Anniversary Celebration ad in the Syracuse, KS newspaper.[118]

138

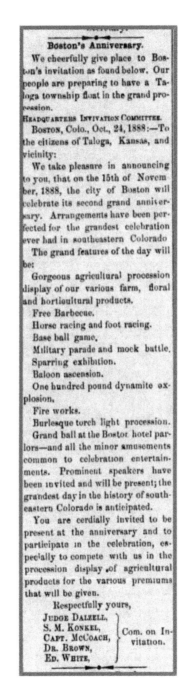

Boston's Anniversary.

We cheerfully give place to Boston's invitation as found below. Our people are preparing to have a Taloga township float in the grand procession.

HEADQUARTERS INVITATION COMMITTEE.

BOSTON, Colo., Oct., 24, 1888:—To the citizens of Taloga, Kansas, and vicinity:

We take pleasure in announcing to you, that on the 15th of November, 1888, the city of Boston will celebrate its second grand anniversary. Arrangements have been perfected for the grandest celebration ever had in southeastern Colorado

The grand features of the day will be:

Gorgeous agricultural procession display of our various farm, floral and hortioultural products.

Free Barbecue.

Horse racing and foot racing.

Base ball game.

Military parade and mock battle.

Sparring exhibition.

Baloon ascension.

One hundred pound dynamite explosion.

Fire works.

Burlesque torch light procession.

Grand ball at the Boston hotel parlors—and all the minor amusements common to celebration entertainments. Prominent speakers have been invited and will be present; the grandest day in the history of southeastern Colorado is anticipated.

You are cordially invited to be present at the anniversary and to participate in the celebration, especially to compete with us in the procession display of agricultural products for the various premiums that will be given.

Respectfully yours,

JUDGE DALZELL,
S. M. KONKEL,
CAPT. McCOACH,   } Com. on In-
DR. BROWN,   vitation.
ED. WHITE,

Boston's Second Anniversary Celebration ad in the Taloga, KS newspaper [119]

139

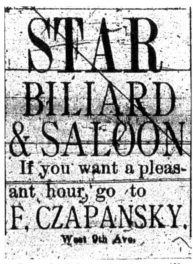

Capansky Saloon advertisement.[120]

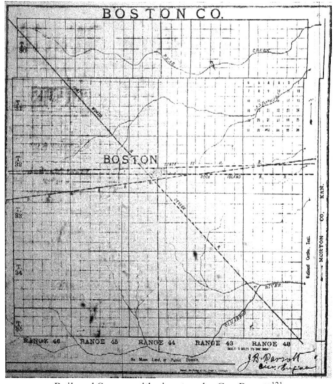

Railroad Survey with signature by Cap Parrott[121]

Chapter 11: Open Range

"**The largest herd of cattle I ever saw was in the summer of 1888. It stretched north from the mouth of Leon Creek, 25 miles southwest of the present Clayton (New Mexico) for 5 or 6 miles. It was accompanied by 2 crews of 12 men each. Cattle belonging in Southern Colorado and the Cimarron River country to the estimated number of 15,000 head made up this great mass of cows, fresh branded calves and steers -- old and young -- which were being moved to their home ranges. At night the stock was loose guarded. It was too bulky to close up. In this herd were cattle bearing brands of the Prairie Company, the Western Land and Cattle Company (101's) and the Muscatine Cattle Company, all Scotch companies.**"

- Albert W. Thompson

The Prairie Cattle Company was established in December of 1880 with headquarters in Edinburgh, Scotland. The initial investors noticed that the ranching business had assumed extensive proportions in the Western States and territories of America and had yielded very large profits, in spite of the fact that these activities were carried out by persons of limited means which were thus subject to many disadvantages. The Prairie Cattle Company intended to change that formula.

The original proposition for embarking upon the enterprise connected with the western cattle range business was first introduced in
Edinburgh by the Underwood, Clark, and Company in 1880. At the
time the knowledge of the western range business of America was
only known to Scotsman by way of romance. It was represented to
the people in Scotland as an industry whereby all they had to do was
to put their money into cattle, which could graze upon the western
prairie grass free of any cost, and then be sent to the market fat. The
proposition submitted by Underwood, Clark, and Company to a few
financial men in Edinburgh included the purchase of a ranch in Colorado and in New Mexico and afterwards a ranch in Texas. A
company was constituted in January, 1881 with a board of directors.
The original issued capital of the company was 100,000 pounds, but
this was increased during the two or three years following for the purpose of adding additional herds of cattle. The theory submitted to the
financial circle, and afterwards to the shareholders was by purchasing
patches of land up and down the water courses in Colorado, the owners of this land, having access to the water, would be able to control
the whole range of the district. The intention of this theory was that
by investing a comparatively small amount in land, the shareholders
would have the benefit of unlimited grazing rights around the land

with water. This theory gains importance when discussing the regulator later on and how the Prairie Company ensured access to water for their cattle was not limited.

The enormity of the foreign owned cattle companies of the American west cannot be over stated. The Prairie Cattle Company was the first and the biggest but Albert W. Thompson tells us,

Of the great cattle ranches of the 1880's and 90s in the 'Strip,' several were foreign incorporated. Six miles down the Cimarron from the line of New Mexico, the Western Land and Cattle Company, Scotch owned, had, in the early '80's, established its 101 ranch. Ten miles below the 101's was the OX's, owned by Towers and Gudgel, Americans. Further east ten miles, sufficient distance to prevent crowding, was the Muscatine Cattle Company's headquarters, the ZH's, while on the north Carrizo, a tributary of the Cimarron, were smaller cattle owner enterprises, several of which large enough to warrant running round up wagons in summer and fall, with whom the "little fellow" worked while gathering his stock and branding his calves. Other large operators were the XYZ's and Pitchforks, which ranged near the headwaters of the Cimarron."[122]

Forty miles up the Cimarron and across the line of New Mexico were the Cross L headquarters, one of three divisions of the largest cattle operation of them all, the Prairie Cattle Company, Ltd.

In 1881 W. R. Green visited the Cross L ranch for the purpose of buying them out for the Prairie Cattle Company. He was driven from Trinidad in an ambulance driven by 4 horses where the owners met him. He spent several days looking over the range and cattle.

The purchase of the Cross L began the story of what is called the most colossal livestock venture ever launched in the American west during the days of free range cattle. The presence of the Prairie Cattle Company, their methods of dealing with livestock thieves, and the inevitable pressures caused by homesteaders and town builders such as the Atlantis Town Company are forever intertwined with the demise of Boston.

To gain perspective on how large the Prairie outfit was, begin with the fact that they had three ranch divisions. Division No. 1 had headquarters at the JJ Ranch in Higbee, Colorado. Division No. 2, which we already mentioned was at the Cross L in Clayton, New Mexico and Division No. 3 at the LIT or Littlefield Ranch at Channing, Texas. Although numerous smaller operations were also purchased it was under the brands of these three ranches that the Prairie operated and it was these three in conjunction with the numerous smaller purchases that created the 300 mile north south expanse of this giant cattle venture.

When the JJ was purchased in 1882 its brand became identified with this huge operation, but it was purchased along with seven other Colorado ranches. Again that was just a portion of their overall U.S. investment. Add in New Mexico, Texas and the Neutral strip they controlled from north to south 300 miles of cattle country from the Arkansas River to the Canadian River. From East to West, Kansas to the Rockies, the Prairie Cattle Company was really, really, really big.

In southeast Colorado, discussion of the Prairie Company and the JJ Cattle Company were often intermingled with each other. Although other ranches were purchased at the same time the JJ was the largest of the Colorado Cattle outfits purchased by the Prairie Cattle Company and the brand under which they operated.

Prairie Cattle Company Brands[123]

Chapter 12: The Regulator

"That there was little difference between the bad man and the good man who went out after him was frequently demonstrated in the early roaring days of the West. The religion of progress and civilization meant very little to the Western town marshal, who sometimes, or often, was a peace officer chiefly because he was a good fighting man."

–Emerson Hough, 1907

The enormity of the Prairie Cattle Company brought with it certain complications. The lawless state of the Neutral Strip enhanced the complications. The Strip as it was called then was no one's domain. One fellow had as much right to settle within it as another. Outlaws and fugitives from justice could camp at a spring or a water hole, erect a crude cabin and begin their nefarious vocation of burning brands, killing livestock and driving strays and other livestock across the line into Kansas or Colorado. Whenever a settler got "beef hungry" he roped and killed the fattest cow or steer he could find on the range and no questions were asked. How would these gigantic foreign corporations even know they had lost one beef? But as cattle stealing became too general and common, the large companies thought it time to stop the practice. A pool was formed and a detective employed, whose business was to ferret out and arrest thieves and undesirables. The stockmen's protective pool employed William "Bill" Thompson, as the guardian of the range. Thompson had punched cows, was handy with a gun and was fearless. Although he worked for many cattle outfits through the cattlemen's protective pool, he is most noted for being an employee of the Prairie Cattle Company. At different times he carried the title regulator, deputy sheriff, killer, cattle detective and dance hall owner. He also went by these names: William Thompson, Will Thompson, Bill Thompson, and Big Bill Thompson. Some even say Bill Thompson was an alias and that his real name was "Charlye Hall" or "Mason" and that he may have been from Texas.[124] [125] However, most evidence points to his name actually being Bill Thompson and that he was from Kansas.

He is not to be confused with Uncle Bill Thompson, Baca County Pioneer who is mentioned when Konkel writes about brothers Gid and Bill Thompson later. For clarity in understanding the difference between the two different Bill Thompsons, we will call the regulator, "Big Bill Thompson" and the Baca County Pioneer, "Uncle Bill Thompson." It should be noted this is not the brother of the famous gunfighter Ben Thompson who also had a brother named Bill who was known to be handy a firearm. Albert W. Thompson, long time editor of the Clayton, New Mexico newspaper who also encountered Big Bill, and who is referenced throughout this narrative is no relation to either Big Bill or Uncle Bill.

Understanding the method by which the Prairie Cattle Company controlled the range as described in the previous chapter provides a picture of how settlers coming into southeast Colorado might interrupt the the plans of Prairie company if any fences were built which would impede Prairie Company cattle from gaining access to the water which they controlled. Taking care of such actions by homesteaders became part of Big Bill Thompson's job and at least one part of his job was simple, ensuring Prairie Cattle Company livestock could get to water. This leads us to Southeastern Colorado's view of the regulator Big Bill Thompson. There was a degree of contempt for the company and the local lore of Big Bill Thompson in southeast Colorado paints him, quite simply as a cold-blooded killer or executioner of homesteaders.

The southeast Colorado prairie is dotted with ruins of homesteads whose occupants were reported to have been executed by Thompson. The most accessable of these ruins is the old homestead near the Crack Cave entrance in Picture Canyon Colorado west of present-day Campo, Colorado. This is just one example of a family Big Bill executed because of the water near the location and water was always a need for the Prairie Cattle Company. The other homesteads of murdered pioneers also had live water or springs nearby.

Albert W. Thompson says of the regulator,

"Bill Thompson as I met him in 1889, was a florid cheeked,
stocky man, weighing I should judge 240 pounds. His eyes were
black. He wore no coat. A vest covered his chest and a rotound
stomach. A single 45 hung from his hip." [126]

During the time he was employed by the Prairie Cattle Company,
it is reported the company secured for him a position of a deputy
sheriff of Las Animas County, Colorado. Boston was a favorite
stomping grounds for Thompson and various regulators who rode
with him, much to the dismay of the local citizens. Most often
mentioned as riding with Thompson are Ben Darnell, Ed Maxwell and
Bill Rowan. Others listed as riding with Thompson at various times
include Kid Doss, Big John Dick, and Harry Overby. Thompson
more than any other individual is tied to the history and demise of
Boston.

The only known picture of Big Bill Thompson was taken at the event above, a picture commonly known as "A Cowboy Funeral" There were at least a couple of cow boys integral to the history of Old Boston in this picture. When counting left to right in the photo, Bill Thompson and Ben Darnell are cow boys number 19 and 20 respectively. Albert Thompson says of this 1891 event,

"Without a preacher a cowhand was laid to rest near a ranch, people coming miles to the obsequies, their nearest town a hundred miles distant. The dead, coffin being unattainable, was wrapped in the canvas of his bedroll, and a Bible being obtained, the wagon boss of the deceased read a few verses." [128]

Emerson Hough in his 1907 work, "The Story of the Outlaw" says about desperados of the American West such as Big Bill,

"As to knowing him, the only way was by trying him. His reputation, true or false, just or unjust, became the herald of the bad man in due time. The 'killer' of a Western town might be

---

[8] NOTE: The author's grandma taught in a one room school (Carrizo Springs School) a couple miles east of this location.

known throughout the state or in several states. His reputation might long outlast that of able statesmen and public benefactors. "

This is true about Big Bill. Unlike the stories of many of the people in the Boston story which faded away, Thompson's reputation is still alive in local lore. We have more to say about Big Bill Thompson later in discussing the siege of Boston, but for now Sam Konkel recalls the following:

The leader of the cow boys was one Bill Thompson. At the time and various times in the employ of the Prairie Cattle Co., the company securing him for the position of deputy marshal.

Just what else Bill Thompson did for a living, or whether anything else or not, nobody knew. He would stay in Boston for days at a time – often weeks at a time, and often was away two or three months before returning. His and the other so-called cow boys' headquarters were in the Cimmaron – in the so-called "No Man's Land" where at that time outlaws were outside of any court jurisdiction.

Chapter 13: The Deviltry of Boston

"A. J. Kinnear says he don't want to go to Colorado. He's afraid it's a bad place. He says he sold about $75 worth of revolvers and ammunition this week to parties bound for Colorado, and where such paraphernalia are necessary, he don't want to go."

- Clark County Republican, 1887

Boston, Colorado quickly gained a reputation as a wild little town. Even Boston stories without violence had an aura of mystery about them such as the one below.[129]

> WOODSDALE *Democrat:* A lady and gentlemen passed through Woodsdale at a late hour Wednesday night, and from the description of Editor Moore, of St. Louis, who recently eloped with pretty Mrs. Norton, it was thought that it was he who passed through the city. He made inquiry about the road to Boston, Colorado, and seem to be in a considerable of a hurry. The lady who accompanied him was closely veiled, and of course could not be recognized. Both were fashionably dressed, and presented an air of ease and refinement.

If you didn't get shot or lynched in Boston there were many other typical frontier hardships possible as shown in the reports below:

"Henry Bivens of Boston, Colorado, was stung by a centipede Friday night. At last accounts he was still living, but suffering very much. "[130]

"John Gillian, a boy of eleven summers, was bitten by a rattle snake near Boston, Colorado within three miles of his home yesterday. He had the presence of mind to tie his suspenders above the wounded arm and, assisted by his mother, scraped off the poisonous part and it is thought escaped from the deadly effects. "[131]

"We learn through A. N. Fleming, that Geo. Leatherman, formerly of this place, but now of Boston, Colorado, was kicked by a mule recently, breaking his leg in such a manner that amputation was necessary to save his life. "[132]

Often deadly encounters between cow boys working for the various cattle companies in the area and in Boston weren't uncommon, as the following reports attest,

"One cowboy cowardly murdered another who was drunk at Indianapolis, Colo. "[133]

"A saloon keeper of Boston, Colorado, was shot and instantly killed by an unknown man, on the morning of the 23rd." [134]

As was often the case the Jennings were right in the middle of the action. [135]

> Willie Hatchett, of Boston, Colo., was accidentally shot by John Jennings, with a 45-calibre revolver, the ball taking effect just above the wrist and ranging upward, finally lodging in the elbow, shivering the bone and mutilating the flesh in a terrible manner. On the 2nd inst. Drs. Park and Jennings split the flesh so as to enable them to extract the ball and dress the wound.—Vilas Democrat.

We have several examples of churches and ministers being in Boston. However, it did appear to be a rough place for those concerned about matters of faith as this April 4, 1889 notice indicates,

> *"The religious editor who runs the Boston (Colorado) Banner, says, "For five consecutive times now we have been disappointed by the preacher who was announced for services. Some better arrangements are sorely needed."* [136]

The violence occurring in Boston 1886-1889 was beyond the violence of the typical frontier boomtown. Reports such as the following often came from the Kansas towns where many of the Boston settlers originated. [137]

> —John A. Kirk, a somewhat noted sporting character of former days in Wellington, is reported to have been killed recently at Boston, Colorado. He left here about two years since. At one time he was wealthy, but most of his riches took liquid form and ran down his throat.

The wild happenings coming out of Boston were pretty steady throughout its brief existence. Al Jennings 1913 book, *Beating Back*, gives us a brief but colorful overview of the Jennings Clan's time in Boston. Al was often accused of exaggeration but based on all we know about Boston, he may not have been too far off. Jennings writes,

"You will look in vain for Boston on the map. It was one of those boom towns with which the pioneer businessmen of that era shook the dice against fate. If they won, they had the foundation of a future Denver or Oklahoma City; if they lost, the place reverted to a primitive wilderness. Boston lay in the middle of a rich cattle country; but that was not the basis of its bid for prosperity. Las

Animas County, in which it was situated, is a large county. The boomers of Boston planned to divide the county and have Boston for the county seat. They put up a $10,000 Hotel and a street of stores; they laid out a town site and grew rich on paper trading lots; and they pulled all their ready money in to fund a corrupt Colorado legislature, which in those days was easily corruptible. The firm of Jennings Brothers -- Al and Frank – ran a hardware store, opened a real estate office, and pooled their funds with the rest.

Boston shared in the disorder of all towns in the cattle country. The cowboys used to come in from the range on Saturday nights and shoot up Main Street. On one day Boston had three funerals due to the violence.

A settler shot his neighbor. Since it was cold blooded assassination, a band of tougher citizens -- the Jennings Brothers had no part in this-- lynched the murderer. That same afternoon. A bystander, drawing just in time, killed him. The one clergyman in Boston refuse to bury the cowboy. Al Jennings, always a friend of the cattle element, conducted the services over him.

"Told all about his, virtues" says Al, "Didn't take long."

There was another wild night when Judge Jennings, by his courage and eloquence, kept a drunken mob from committing a lynching, before the bottom fell out of Boston."[138]

Various other headlines told of the constant violence in Boston. Alberta Clark, whose parents ran a restaurant on South Main, played a role in the final siege, or what Konkel refers to as the final grand round up. She says of Boston,

> *"I remember Bill Rowan and Joe Tate came to town and got drunk and went to shooting in the livery barn, and one of the bullets came thru our house, clear thru the cupboard and struck the stove, deflecting and burying in the wood box. Mother and we kids were alone and we didn't lose any time getting down in the cellar."*[139]

One of the more widely publicized news stories out of Boston was the lynching of a homesteader which Al Jennings mentioned previously. The story involves two homesteaders, one named Hickman and one named Booth or Boothe. Konkel writes,

Judge Lynch on the Job
About three or four miles north of Boston lived Cornelius Hickman, and a few miles away from a man by the name of Boothe.

Hickman was a widower without children, while Boothe was a bachelor, probably close to forty.

The sequel to this judge Lynch story was a widow, Mrs. Nevel, who is nesting with Hickman, and to whom Booth was engaged to be married.

Hickman claims the woman was owing to him $300, and he didn t propose to have her carried off till he got his money. He consequently warned Boothe that he would kill him if he didn t stay away.

One evening startling news was received in Boston that a dead man was lying in a wagon off Northeast of town, and it was at once surmised that the man was Boothe.

Two dozen mounted men were soon at the scene of the tragedy and found it to be Booth as supposed. Knowing that Hickman had threatened the fellow's life, the posse preceded at once to his home.

Hickman greeted them very cordially, admitted the killing, and was brought to town and placed in a room in the Boston hotel, with three guards.

The next morning he was given a trial in a justice court, when apparently with a great deal of pride he related the story of the killing, which was as follows:

A fellow by the name of Winecup was living north of Hickman, he had been downtown and was leaving some meat at Hickman s as he went home.

Before reaching the place he met Hickman, who had started to town, but who said he would now turn around and go back home, and suiting the action to the word started off on a keen lope. At the same time he saw Boothe coming on horseback from the east, and surmised it would be trouble.

As Winecup drove up he heard a woman screaming in the house and at the same time Boothe rode up and said, "Let's go in there and find out what that man is doing to that woman," at the same time jumping off his pony.

Just then Hickman rushed out of the house with a shot-gun, one barrel of which was accidentally discharged, he firing the other point blank at Boothe.

Boothe then made a grab for his pony, but it jumped and got away from him. He then jumped into Winecup wagon and drove for his life.

When Hickman got his gun reloaded he jumped on his own horse and started after Boothe. He ran him a mile, caught up with him, held the gun within a few feet of the victim, and while the fellow was begging for his life, dis-charged the gun and tore a hole through the fellow s heart as big as a dollar.

While the trial was going on and Hickman appar-ently was in his glory at relating the circumstances, the grim countenances of the good people listening to the details as told by Hickman himself didn t auger anything good for the murderer.

The man by the justice was bound over to the district court for trial and was returned to the hotel room, with the same guards over him.

Sometime during the night a delegation of probably two dozen armed man came to the fellow s room, "overpowered" the guards and took forcible possession of Hickman. Now realizing they meant business, Hickman fought like a wildcat, and his wheezing could be heard all over the house as he was dragged through the hall and down the stairs.

They dragged and carried him to a vacant building in the north part of town, and there in the morning he was found hanging to a rafter.

When laid in his coffin the markings of the rope were plainly visible on his neck. He was laid to rest in the Boston cemetery, in an unmarked grave, where he will peacefully sleep until called to the presence of a higher court.[140]

The widespread news of the Hickman lynching was in line with Konkel's version with only slight variations. The October 1888 *Aspen Chronicle*, for example, reported the sensational lynching in Boston, Colorado as follows,

"One Hickman was the victim. He had his mistress with him, and got her to prove up on his agricultural claim. Booth was engaged to marry the woman, and called at Hickman's to see her. Hickman drove him from the place at the point of a shot-gun, and shot him when in sight of the house. He was found weltering in his blood, with sixteen buck shot in his body. Seventy five armed men

rode to Hickman's place, took him out to the nearest tree[9], and obtained a confession of the crime from him. They then lynched him in the usual orthodox manner."[141]

At Boston, Colorado, a man named Hickman last week shot and killed J. C. Booth in a quarrel about a woman, and a mob of seventy-five men afterward took Hickman from his house and lynched him.

A MAN named Hickman, living near Boston, Colo., shot and killed one J. C. Booth because of a woman. A mob of 75 men on the 5th took the murderer from his home and lynched him.

Two of many newspaper reports
of this event across the country.[142] [143]

---

[9] Locals and those familiar with the Southeast Colorado plains will find this statement highly unlikely.

162

Although Konkel tells of Booth being a bachelor, the timeline and news reports of the time seem to link the Booth / Hickman incident to the following story:[144]

> Comrade Henry A. Booth, of Lincoln Post, was shot and killed at Boston, Colorado, October 6. His widow has just returned from that place, where she went to get his personal effects. She found parties there wearing his watch, chain, and ring, and they also had his trunk and clothing, all of which they refused to give the widow, claiming that the coroner's fees and funeral expenses must first be paid. She was unable to pay them and had to return without them. If there was a Grand Army Post there she would have had no trouble.

The murder of Henri "Frenchy Savoy is another locally spread tale of murder from the Boston era and Konkel discusses Savoy in great detail. Alternate spellings of "Henri" and "Savoy" were "Henry and "Savoie," respectively. A lesser known murder possibly connected to the Savoy incident is the murder of John Phillips. Phillips according to some accounts was in a horse-stealing ring with Henry Savoy and Big Bill Thompson. Other sources indicate their family would not have taken such care with John Phillips grave if he had been a horse thief and they feel he may have just been at the wrong place at the wrong time. Whatever the circumstances of the Phillips murder, Ike Osteen, in his book "A Place Called Baca," promotes the idea that the murder of Phillips further intensified the rage of the Boston citizens toward Thompson and the regulators. This theory makes sense as Bostonians weren't too happy with Big Bill and the cow boys anyway.

A 1935 interview with Baca County Pioneer Uncle Bill Thompson provides the following account of the Savoy murder and how John Phillips is connected,

"The killing of Savoy appears to have occurred after Big Bill Thompson brought him in and left the cell where he was being kept unlocked. Big Bill, and Savoy were in on stealing horses together and of all the cattle and horse thieves, Big Bill was the biggest. Another man named John Phillips, who lived part time in Boston and part time in the Neutral Strip, was also entangled with Thompson and Savoy in some fashion. Henri Savoy's land lay just south of our land southeast of Vilas. His dugout faced the clump of cottonwoods down on the banks of the Sand Arroyo. The place owned by Gid Thompson's children was formerly called Wild Horse Ranch. It belonged to Ben Gilliam, who was married to Frenchy's sister. Frenchy was Henri Savoy's nickname. It was here on the Sand Arroyo that Frenchy lived and rustled cattle and horses.

John Phillips sold Uncle Bill a mare for $50. Phillips and Big Bill got into a quarrel over the money in Old Boston. Big Bill demanded his share of the money. The fuss waxed hotter and

hotter. All three men were drinking. Phillips pulled his gun and said,

"We'll settle this with a musket. I sold that horse and Bill[10] does not have to win her back."

Phillips, had a dugout down in one of the canyons near the border of the Neutral Strip. Big Bill Thompson was afraid of Phillips, for he was a pretty game fellow, so when Phillips called his hand, Big Bill laughed it off, tho Frenchy continued to argue.

Uncle Bill said, when outlaws go to fighting among themselves it sure meant death to somebody. About a week later Big Bill went down to Squaw Canyon and spent the night with Phillips. About a week later Phillips was found dead in his front yard. All of his stock was gone and a certain outlaw had them in his possession with fictitious bills of sale. Some of those horses had come into Phillips possession honestly and others dishonestly. He had gambled away all of the $50.

Later back in Boston Big Bill under his title of Deputy Sheriff arrested Frenchy for stealing from the Cattle Growers Association. With him in custody Thompson accidently, so it is said, left the door unlocked. Frenchy walked out of the room and Big Bill shot him. He later claimed Frenchy was trying to escape.

---

[10] This refers to Uncle Bill Thompson, not Big Bill Thompson. Big Bill didn't like someone getting the upper hand on him and this very well may have set off Big Bill for the eventual murder of Phillips.

Frenchy is buried 150 yards from the Thompson homestead southeast of Vilas.[145]

John Phillips Grave in the present day Oklahoma Panhandle.
The photo is by the author.

Sam Konkel writes of the Savoy murder,

The Killing of Savoy

Our readers will remember the mention of Henry Savoy in an early chapter of these write-ups, the man who rode up to our camp on our first morning in Colorado and wanted to know if we had seen "his horses."

Savoy had a human habitation on the south banks of the Sandy Arroyo, at the point where the water, by the nature of underlying stratum is brought close to the surface, and the cottonwoods shade the ground with great tops, in the neighborhood where Gid and Bill Thompson live now.

In the bottom of the creek bed was a hole dug in the sand, with a dry goods box in the hole that watered the whole country round-about until wells could be put down. The spring was six miles north of where we and our folks were located and from it we hauled water during the summer and fall.

Savoy had a wife and some broncs, probably home-made furniture in the house, we believe had some kind of driving vehicle, and so far as we know, now he may have had a cow or two, and possibly some chickens although we don t at this time recall seeing any.

How he lived nobody knew, but of course living was cheap in those days, and a sack of flour costing 90 cents would carry himself and wife 2 or 3 months, and antelope and small game would do the rest.

We have told you something of Bill Thompson the cow boy whose home was somewhere on the Cimarron in the neutral strip

So far as we know, the only thing Bill ever did in his life was to drink whiskey and to draw money as some kind of deputy sheriff, the appointment to which was secured for him by the Prairie Cattle Company.

Bill was sometimes deputy marshal and sometimes a deputy sheriff, and in one of these capacities, he had two or three times arrested Savoy for stealing JJ cattle.

Whether Savoy killed any JJ s for home consumption we are not able to say, but we think it improbable that he did for selling purposes, as he never sold any meat at Boston or anywhere else, so far as anything was ever told of it, or accusations made.

> Stock Breeder: On complaint of Murdo McKenzie, manager Prairie Cattle company, Henry Savoy, of Boston, Col., is under indictment for getting away with a Prairie company cow. It is believed this will furnish a chain of evidence to convict others and put a stopper on the wholesale live live stock stealage so rampant of late in Southern Colorado.

Notice of Henry Savoy stealing Prairie Company cows. [146]

The JJs though went on the principle that as the boy had no income, he must be living off their cattle, and Bill Thompson was probably not too particular about the kind of trap used to catch him.

So once more Bill had Savoy under arrest, and was holding him prisoner at the Boston Hotel-- held there we believe by a raging blizzard. Our recollection is that it was during holidays. Anyway, Savoy wanted to go uptown for a smoke or a drink, or something; and Bill told him that he would take him up.

They went up and got what he wanted and started back. What happened on the way back no mortal knew except those two -- except Savoy got a bullet through one side near the lungs.

Bill Thompson said Savoy started to run away, and he was consequently forced to shoot him.

On the contrary, Savoy made a dying statement under oath that they were walking along quietly together when Bill suddenly faced about and shot him down.

However the situation really occured, Boston believed the Savoy story, and believed Bill had shot him down in cold blood.

Immediately after the killing, Bill left Boston, and as there had been a good deal of loud talk of what the Thompson gang was going to get, it was presumed that Bill was so badly scared he would never come back.

The grand jury sitting in the following March found an indictment against Bill Thompson for the murder in the first degree; but we do not know what disposition was made of the case, further than that he was never punished for the crime.

As already intimated but not definitely stated, Savoy, after a lingering illness of something like a couple of weeks, passed in his chips and had them cashed; and he has ever since been quietly resting in an unmarked grave in the Boston Cemetery.[11]

And Bill Thompson-- we are not through with him yet. He didn t stay away from Boston though it was generally supposed he would and consequently figures in on a general round of the town, following a citizen's effort to everlastingly annihilate the cow boy outfit.[147]

---

[11] NOTE: Savoy is not buried in the Boston Cemetery, but rather on private land.

Chapter 14: Stealing Houses

"Vilas is the name of new town in Las Animas County, Colorado, which boasts of two newspapers, two drug stores and seven saloons." It is probably a good democratic town. No other kind of town would boast of seven saloons to two drug stores."

-Dodge City Times, 1887

Kansas had already seen its share of bloody battles between towns competing for the county seat by the time the Colorado town boom began. Such experience with the bloody fights spawned speculation about what was about to happen in Colorado between competing towns.

"Two Coldwater companies have located towns in Las Animas county Colorado, and a long and bitter fight will probably occur. One town company composed of Judge Jennings, Treasurer Darroch and others located the town of Boston last fall and gave it something of a boom. Another company composed of Tim Shields, Sam Sisson, H. Chapman and others have recently located the town of Vilas City, said to be eight miles from Boston, and as the company is composed of twenty five members and each member will build two or three buildings, and the company will build a large hotel and other buildings, it will soon attract large attention

*and be a formidable rival of Boston. There is lots of fun ahead for somebody. – **Coldwater Review** "*[148]

As towns were attempting to grow quickly in the boomtown days they would buy houses or buildings from one town to move to another. Sometimes this movement involved an outright purchase of buildings and sometimes incentives such as town lots were offered to building owners to move from one town to another. Often there were howls of protest and even violence. This move of buildings from Richfield, Kansas to Boston, Colorado was the first effort of this kind in the area and seemed to be one of the more peaceful events of this kind.[149]

> ## We understand that Richfield is moving her buildings to Boston, Colo.

They were watching the Colorado county seat fights unfold as far away as California. The September 8, 1888 issue of the *Oakland California Tribune* tells a different story about the conflict for a new county seat and the removal of houses from Vilas to Boston:

> *We have had something to say heretofore about the remarkable County Seat Wars which have been so often marked by bloodshed in Kansas and Colorado in the past 2 years. The wars*

are not always bloody, however, and sometimes assumed a com-
mercial aspect. This is the case of the two rival towns of Boston
and Vilas in Colorado, now engaged in the struggle of this sort.
The towns are 12 miles apart in Eastern Las Animas County.
Early last spring the town of Stonington was established 6 miles
east of Boston and 18 miles from Vilas. With characteristic en-
terprise it immediately started to "do up" its nearest rival,
Boston, by quietly buying some of her buildings and moving them
over on wheels. The buying was not such a hard matter, but the
moving was. The people of Boston did not "catch on" to the
move until a good size building was placed on wheels and horses
were attached to it. Then they came out in force and compelled
the Stonington people to go home. The Stonington man came the
next day with increased force, but found an armed guard await-
ing them, and got so many minutes to retreat from the town
uninjured. About 2 months after this Boston tried the same tactic
of house moving from Vilas, and was unsuccessful. In as much as
they could not complain. For the last 3 months neither town has
been doing much in the plan was entered into where by the Two
Towns might be consolidated. For certain interest in the town of
Boston, Chockley, the Vilas banker, two merchants, and about 20
families agreed to transfer their buildings and business to Bos-
ton. The other citizens of Vilas refused to compromise in that
manner, and swore they would not allow the others to go. The pa-
triots were foiled, however, and the buildings were removed

without bloodshed. Chockley, was arrested by the order of Mayor Crossman of Vilas, on the charge of defacing buildings. On trial he was released by the police magistrate. Four times was the banker arrested on various charges, but each time he was released. Chockley went to Boston and there swore out a warrant for the arrest of Mayor Crossman and Marshall McIntyre on the charge of assault with intent to do bodily harm. Vilas, heard of it and sent down word the man or men who undertook to make the arrest would be killed.

Here circumstances became interesting. Ten picked men were deputized to make the arrest. Leaving Boston at midnight they arrived at Vilas at three in the morning. Their armed deputies went to Crossman's room in the hotel, a portion went for McIntyre and the others remained on guard. The mayor resisted the deputies amid the shrieks of the women in the hotel and the general hubbub of which the arrival of the invaders had caused. Both parties finally found resistance useless and gave themselves up. On trial the mayor was released and the marshal was bound over to wait for seating for the grand jury. Boston said she will have every vestige of Vilas moved and the latter decidedly says she will not be moved so the matter rests for the present.[150]

The final battle in the naming of the county was not yet finished. Konkel writes the following,

Moving Houses from Vilas to Boston

An east ender positively asserts that 47 houses in Vilas will be moved to Boston - *Trinidad Daily Citizen*

Five houses have already been moved, three more will positively come and about 40 are under consideration - **Boston** *Western World*

Last week five houses and several of the best citizens of Vilas moved to Boston. The Vilas Democrat comes out calling the parties who moved all kinds of names, and in consequence, the owners were arrested for criminal libel - *Richfield (Kans.) Republican.*

When at its best Vilas was a very beautiful town, we believe in this respect having the edge on any of the other towns, and it was second in size and population.

But Vilas was almost wholly void of diplomats, quite different in this respect to Boston, Springfield, and Minneapolis. Bob Crossman was its principal asset in this line, but he was no match in the cleverness to the Ringlings of the other towns and hence Vilas never did cut much of a figure in the county-seat affairs of the east end.

Captain John McCoach, a kind of one-horse lawyer, was the first to come from Vilas to Boston. All he had to bring with him was his clothes and a napsack or something of the kind, but it was largely through Cap. McCoach that the house-moving arrangements were made.

The Boston town company had a lot of town lots at its disposal, and Mr. McCoach acting as a mediator, got a number of Vilas people to agree to move down inclusive of their bankrupt banker and several others and five houses.

Of course, Vilas became greatly excited and took an oath to the heathen gods that a young graveyard would be started when Boston undertook to pull a house out of their town.

Accordingly on a certain day probably 100 men with shotguns, Winchesters and other argumentative weapons, a justice of the peace, two constables, the town marshal, and the necessary team force, hired themselves to Vilas to possess themselves of those houses and to convey the same without unnecessary delay and by the shortest route from said Vilas to the said town of Boston, all in the county of (Las Animas at that time) and the state of Colorado.

We don't know whether Vilas had any organization, either for offensive or defensive purposes; but if they did they evidently weren't prepared for a mob of 100 men, and as the law was clearly on the side of the invading army, the angry townsmen could do nothing but watch the proceedings from the safe retreat of their inner sanctuaries.

One hundred men can do a whole lot of work in a short time, and probably in three or four hours after getting on the job the houses were slowly moving out of town and towards their new but not last resting place.

The caravan bivouacked on the north banks of the historic Sandy Arroyo, half the men keeping watch the first part of the night, and the other half the last part of it.

It was after the Hugo-Woodsdale tragedy in No Man's land, spoken of in a former chapter. And those 100 fellows didn't purpose to furnish a second chapter to that bloody affair, with themselves as the party of the second part.

The night drug in length into the following day as if nothing unusual was on tap and with everything quiet on the Potomac.

The next day the houses duly deposited on the lots it had been assigned to there in Boston, and one of the greatest diplomatic strokes of the war was brought to a successful conclusion.

More next week[151]

The Vilas Democrat -- Bob Crossman -- came up with a libelous editorial on the parties moving from their town, and proceedings were immediately brought against the said Bob to even things up a little.

Bob was brought to Boston a time or two or three to stand trial, but getting a changed venue the case was finally dropped.

All this happened in August 1888, when a county seat for Boston was supposed to be a sure thing. But, as you know --The best-laid plans of mice and men often go astray.

The county seat went awry, and the country went to the dogs, and those houses and all the other houses in Boston, and all the other towns of Baca excepting Springfield and Vilas were pulled here and there into the country.

Vilas when we last saw it in the old days was something as shown in the photo view of in printed elsewhere in the paper.[152]   Fifteen years later on our return to Baca we found Vilas with half a dozen houses, all but one or two owned by Baca County's only merchant outside of Springfield.

Also, Boston was all there when the writer took his plan out of the doomed city in the old days. Then fifteen years later on our return to the old town there was nothing but piles of stone and holes in the ground to tell of its one-time greatness.

Thus the moving of the five houses didn't cut much of figure anyway, the towns of the whole east end being doomed to go down together -- the county seat along with the rest of them.[153]

The photo above would be prior to 1905 as the two story Vilas hotel, on the left, burned in 1905. The building on the right with the round topped false front was a saloon that was moved to Vilas after the demise of Boston. That building is the only one left from the Boom town era and is in Vilas, Colorado.[154]

Chapter 15: A Fight for the County Seat

"Five town site declaratory statements were filed in the Lamar land office last week. They all had courthouse squares."

-*Buena Vista Democrat*, 1887

It is a cold day when some new town doesn't start up in Southeastern Colorado. In the short space of four months, there have been seventeen towns laid out south of the railroad and east of Trinidad. They are in the order of their ages ⸺ Boston, Albany, Vilas, Carrizo, Springfield, Minneapolis, Humbar, York, Farmington, Wilde, Holmes, Indianapolis, Athens, Bloomington, Brookfield, Plymouth, and Randal ⸺ *Western World,* April 21, 1887

Without exception, town companies came to southeast Colorado with the idea their town would be the county seat. The battle for county seat honors would be the big fight in 1887-1889.

An 1888 letter to the *"Trinidad Colorado Citizen"* expresses the desire for the east enders of Las Animas County to support a new county seat because of the inconvenience in taking care of required business. They mention the fears surrounding a Kansas style county seat fight, the expense, and the time consumed in traveling 150 miles to conduct business. They stated,

"add to these the physical strain upon the health and energies of one who pulls out of a cold morning to make a stagecoach travel of 80 mile that day to reach the railroad station, or travel 150 miles overland, sleeping out of nights, and eating stale food, and the reader can form some faint idea of our situation."[155]

Emphasizing his point, the writer of the letter above continues by noting that Las Animas County then had more square miles than Connecticut or Rhode Island or New Jersey and was almost as large as Massachusetts. He also warned that subdividing counties could initiate a disastrous county seat war as he had experienced such bitter contests in western Kansas, many people were not predisposed toward subdividing the county."[156]

Another "East End Settler" advocated making three or four counties out of the eastern extremity of Las Animas. He claimed, this would satisfy a majority of the settlers and give several places the chance to become county seat towns. That, he said would stave off county-seat wars, Kansas style. At a meeting in Springfield, the advice was accepted, and four new counties were proposed.[157]

James Church, who ultimately became the first county clerk of Baca County, worked for the Springfield contingent in getting the new

county seat. He may have been the most shrewd of all the people involved in the county seat fight when you read what he said about the
idea of small counties as follows,

> *"Springfield was located concerning natural advantages,*
> *and also to catch the county seat of East County which would*
> *form by making one cut North and South off the east end of*
> *Las Animas County. Colorado seems to be against small*
> *counties, and the laws favor speculation less than in Kan-*
> *sas."[158]*

Every town felt they would be the new county seat of a new
county. As actual building of the towns slowed, the town leaders
used their respective newspapers to ramp up the rhetoric about their
town's qualifications for the county seat and launch attacks on their
competing towns. Everyone knew what was at stake in the coming
election year.

A February 1888 Western World response to a Springfield Herald assertion that Boston "was afraid to compete for the county seat" was met with the following response from Sam Konkel,

The *Western World* 23rd: The insinuation of the *Springfield Herald* that Boston is afraid to "compete" with that little villa for the county seat, if not rich, is certainly the most amusing and ludicrous twaddle. Boston is about as afraid of competing with Omaha or Joliet. When cutting becomes necessary, Boston will be on hands with an ugly looking county carver clinched in its brawny hands, and woe be unto him who standeth not aside.

Boston right now has nearly as great a settlement around it as Springfield, Vilas, and Minneapolis put together, if indeed it has not a greater; and this will more than proportionately increase during the coming year. The facts of the settlement are indisputable, as proven by last fall's election, and as shown by the settlements themselves. The election showed Springfield's fighting weight to be 91 pounds, and Boston's fighting weight to be 257 pounds – a pygmy pitted against a giant."[159]

COLORADO LETTER.

Boston, Colorado, Jan., 26 1887,

Editors New Era:—Perhaps a short letter from this far away section might be of interest to some of your readers. I am now located in Las Animas county, at the thriving little city of Boston, which was only located and platted on the 26th of last November. At present we have sixty-five houses completed and forty-five more commenced, besides contracts are let for about fifty to be built just as soon as workman can be engaged. The land for one hundred miles in either direction is a nice rolling prairie. The quality of the land cannot be surpassed. Our town is seventeen miles from the Kansas line, and is sure to be the county seat of Las Animas county. We will have two railroads just as soon as they can be built. We have at present a tri-weekly stage that runs to Richfield Kansas and makes connections with the railroad. The climate here is the finest in the world. There has not been a day this winter that a man would need an overcoat, and for the past two weeks every one has been at work in their shirt sleeves. Will say to those who contemplate coming west, that this is the coming metropolis. It has no rivals.

Joseph E. Hunter.

Another optimistic report states Boston "is sure to be the county seat of Las Animas County".[160]

The Boston contingent was less aware of the Colorado tendency toward larger counties. The town founders were confident that Boston would become county seat. The map below shows Baca County in 1889 with a glaring mistake showing Boston, Colorado as the county seat.[161]

Sam Konkel provides us greater insight into the county seat fights entangling Boston, Springfield, Vilas, and Minneapolis:

Tioga County

Probably there are not many and possibly not any of the old-timers in Baca County who remember "Tioga County."

It is just barely possible that most of those directly concerned about it and connected with it would remember Tioga County only after having their attention called to the events of those old days that left Boston out in the cold, and finally resulted in the disintegration and scatter-ment of the town to the four winds of the earth.

It was down at Trinidad that most of the conspiracies of those old days were hatched and it was there that Tioga County had its birth. The Democrats were then the majority party in old Las Animas County, and had been for many years, and three or four democrats of Trinidad and all those old days practically constituted the Democratic Party of the county.

Judge Jennings - lawyer, doctor, politician and orator - the weasel of the east end, Albert Hughes president of the Town company and a good second to Jennings in wire manipulations and cunningness, arranged the county seat matters with the "powers" at Trinidad under which arrangements, A. Hughes was supposed to be sent to the legislature from the east end and of course the election of Hughes meant Boston for the county seat.

Doctor Brown always called "Doc" was the paternal progenitor of the name "Tioga," intended as the name to be applied to the intended cut off from the east end of Las Animas. "Tioga" was the name of the county in New York he came from and Doc's influence with the republicans was needed to call the new county Tioga.

Incidents of the County Seat Fights

The incidents wrapped up in the history of Tioga County, of course, belonged to the scheme of making Boston the county seat of whatever was cut off the east end.

When the plan was consummated to send Hughes to the legislature, the Western World mildly opposed his nomination, particularly because of his occasional relapses from the strict state of sobriety and, partly out of the fear of last-minute treachery.

It was argued though by practically everyone that Hughes interests in Boston were so great that no opposing interest could afford to buy him and that consequently he would be the safest man in that respect and could be sent to Denver.

Everybody would rather have had some other safe man, but everything else considered, about everybody thought it unwise to turn him down, and reluctantly the World also joined in support of Hughes for the legislative nomination.

The Convention at Trinidad

It was in the usual convention month when four wagon loads of plug hatted Bostonians, inclusive of the Boston band, drove into the town of Trinidad at the end of three days' overland trip from Boston, and then took possession of the best chuck house in town, ready for the next day's doings.

On the morning of the convention the Boston boys marched double file to the convention hall, preceded by the splendid little band that helped to make Boston famous, and surmounted by the plug hats that were intended to make the boys of the other towns look like 30 cents.

As the nomination at the convention for the east-end representative was supposed to almost settle the county seat controversy each of the towns of the east end had its candidate for the coveted prize.

Hughes as already stated was the Boston choice, McNeal the Minneapolis man, Bob Crossman the Vilas selection and Church for Springfield.

The Mexicanos.

Probably nine-tenths of the delegates at the convention were Mexicans. The white delegates were mostly inside the railing or on the platform, along with a few boss Mexicans.

We believe McNeal was the first put in the nomination, then Crossman, then Church, and the last Hughes.

We believe McNeal was engaged in real estate, became a notary, and afterwards justice of the peace. He made a good talk in his own behalf, and was roundly applauded at the close.

Bob Crossman was our able contemporary at Vilas – wigwagging the *Vilas Democrat,* and at odd times doing law jobs. He made a very able talk when called upon to tell why sentence should be passed on him, and was also heartily applauded in closing.

Jim Church was Springfield's banker and chief monitor. When his time came to tell what excuse he had for getting into the ring and putting on the gloves, he did so satisfactorily and rather plausibly, and was cheered according to the rules of the game.

Convention next week[162]

The convention story is told for the purpose of giving an idea of individuality in some conventions, and in some legislatures also as indicated by the Hughes nomination.

For the purpose of narration of this part of the story, it will be necessary to understand that nine-tenths of the delegates couldn't understand English, and that consequently an interpreter was necessary.

The interpreter was one Sompris, given name not remembered, who was one of the "junta" of Trinidad whose business it was to guide the great democratic craft of the county.

It is worthy to note that of the big Trinidad generals of the democratic part of the county, not one mother's son of them could make a public speech, while the east end had its dozens of public talkers and some that could be classed as orators.

Though he couldn't make a public talk to save his gizzard--or thought he couldn't, interpreter Sopris was as fine an elocutionist as one would usually hear as a public reader; in his interpretations giving the necessary emphasis and gestures to make the address of the other man impressive and effective.

The candidates of the other towns made their little talks, just as if the dice weren't loaded and their talks would have some effect; but when Hughes got up and before he said anything, the interpreter said,

"This is the man you want to vote for."

That was all. The Mexican delegates had their clue, and when the ballot was taken every Mexican vote was for Albert Hughes. That Clue--"this is the man you want to vote for," would have elected a Hotentot or a Zulu in that convention of Mexican puppets.

The Election at Boston

The east end wasn't much of a factor, but at the same time, its favors were courted. So along in October half a dozen of the Trinidad bosses came over to Boston to electioneer, and took in all the east-end towns.

In order to get Minneapolis and Springfield, an arrangement was planned between Boston and Minneapolis and Springfield for the formation of three counties, making each a county seat. For this purpose parts of Prowers and Bent were to be incorporated in the new counties.

By this plan, these three towns apparently worked harmoniously together through the campaign.

That was before the days of Austrailanism, hence the ballot box was easily tampered with. We don't know how it was done at other voting places, but we are presuming that the fear of the Lord, as in the case of Boston, didn't weigh heavily upon any of those towns, and those directly in charge of the election might consequently have been without an overpowering grace, in which case the being may not have been very close to the line of righteousness.

We believe at Boston that Hughes carried the election by some-thing over a five-hundred majority. The other feller--meaning the republican candidate, was allowed to have a few, enough to partly hide things.

A great many people, had already gone from the county, and just how many votes were cast will probably never be known, but probably 300 or 400. The Jenningses had gotten themselves conveniently appointed as ballot-box manipulators. Just how much it was really manipulated is, of course, a matter of guess, but under the circumstances most any kind of a guess wouldn't be far from the mark.

Hughes elected

The county of Las Animas was at that time overwhelmingly democratic, hence the matter of ballot box manipulation would anyway make but little difference in the final results.

The entire democratic county ticket was elected --Albert Hughes for representative and Casemiro Barilla[12] for senator and these two were supposed to be able to swing the county-cutting and county-seat matter whatever way they pleased.

At Denver

The fight was now transferred to Denver. Boston had its representative, and presumedly the support of Senator Barilla. In addition, Dr. Brown was sent as a lobbyist to assist Hughes and Barilla in the building of the southeastern empire.

The other towns -- Minneapolis, Vilas, and Springfield each had its lobbyists at Denver and each looking after its own particular interests.

We believe there was no bill introduced along the lines on which Boston, Minneapolis, and Springfield worked together during the campaign--for the creation of three

---

[12] NOTE: Barilla should be spelled Barela.

counties. Whatever sincerity there was in this plan in the first place, no doubt it didn't take long to find out at Denver that such a formation of counties was out of the question, and that it would be useless to introduce such a bill.

"Tioga" next week[163]

The state legislature was at that time as has always been-- run by less than a dozen persons.

In the very early part of the session, the bill looking to the formation of a county out of the east end of Las Animas was introduced, providing for the present county of Baca, only under the name of Tioga.

The introduction of the bill, of course, eliminated Min- neapolis and by its provision of making Boston the county seat, of course, also eliminated Springfield.

The fight consequently was Boston against the field, with every indication that Boston had only one chance in a probable thousand of losing out.

The bill was read and ordered printed. After a lapse of time, it was read again, according to the rules of the game.

In the last days of the session it was read a third time and passed, it being immediately ratified by the Senate, and went to thence to the governor.

Now comes the phenomenal incidence in connection with this phenomenal Tioga County.

After a few days, the governor returned the bill without his objections--to have some technical corrections made to its wording.

What the technical change wanted we do not now re-call, but it had no relation to a change in the county seat or the name of the county.

We will say candidly that we believe Senator Barilla to be responsible for what then happened to that bill, but is of course only a surmise, with the chance that Ex-Senator Barilla is the only one at the present time that could shed any light on the subject.

But the change made by the legislature was to strike out the word Boston and to substitute Springfield therefore and to change the name Tioga to Baca.

THE governor of Colorado has vetoed the bill establishing Tioga county. As the law now stands, but one county has been created out of Eastern Las Animas county, with Springfield as the county seat. This leaves Boston out in the cold.

News of the new Colorado County[164]

So amended, the bill went back to the governor and was signed by him -- we believe after the legislature had adjourned.

After the first paralyzing news to Boston, the Bostonians wrote the Governor that the old bill rightfully, became a law by the failure of the governor to return it within the prescribed constitutional limits "with his objections."

By the constitution, when a bill goes to the governor, he may return it "with his objections" -- thus vetoing it, and in case he does not sign it, it becomes law after a certain number of days, the same as if it had been by him signed.

Boston was for a short time greatly enthused by this new proposition; but the people were now financially down and out, and as it would take years to grind the thing through the courts for adjustment, the proposition was dropped, and thus the beginning of the end of poor old Boston was in sight.

Of course the county seat elections in 1890 legalized Springfield as the county seat of this county and the lapse of time has legalized the name of Baca; so the whole thing has become a phenomenal anomaly of history, and is referred here only as things that actually were, and the things that really might have been had they been followed up.

The return of Albert Hughes, now branded a traitor by Bostonians generally – Next Week[165]

Hughes Branded Traitor

The editor of the *Western World* was the only one who advised against the nomination of Hughes and was the only one who expressed doubt of his having sold out, and thus having turned traitor to his town and people.

But it was no use. His best friends were the loudest in denouncing him as a traitor, and when he arrived in Boston, we believe a few weeks after the legislature adjourned, he found his good friends either cold or hostile in their attitude and himself consequently suddenly friendless.

That wasn't all he found when he got back to Boston. He had a beautiful residence, with basement and several rooms handsomely furnished -- found in its place a pile of smoldering ashes.

Just who set the building afire no one knew, but all knew instinctively who the instigators were and indirectly responsible for it, and of course in this Hughes shared the general conviction.

The charge made against Hughes was that he sold out to Springfield, accepting Springfield money and property, the latter consisting presumably of several Springfield blocks.

As we saw it, however, Springfield had no more money than was necessary to finance their fight, and if all the vacant lots in town were given to Hughes it would be a small thing compared to his interest in Boston.

A Possible Sequel To the Change in the Bill

As stated before, arrangements had been made with the ramroders at Trinidad for the nomination of Hughes. Whether that included a promise to stand by Boston in the legislature also we do not know, but that would have been a natural part of the understanding.

It was a balmy day sometime after the convention at Trinidad, on a visit of Hughes and Jennings to the town they thought it would be the magnanimous thing to give Hughes the freedom of the city, and so they did.

We do not know what it was that gave rise to the suspicion, but some way or somehow Hughes got it into his noggin that the powers were going to go back on him.

However, we supposed we do know what it was. When a man gets around a certain amount of red-eye, he is primed for a good quantity of overpowering suspicions, whether there is any basis for them or not.

Anyway, Hughes got around both the booze and the suspicion and then made use of the city's freedom by going up and down the streets of the generous town and cussing the "powers" to all that was good and bad, declaring among other things that he was "going hell-bent for the legislature " --powers or no powers.

After having given him the freedom of the city, the ramroders could do nothing but look on with chagrin at the use he was making of it. Of course they were boiling hot at being lampooned as traitors and ingrates, but gritted their teeth and let it go.

The day after, when Hughes had sobered and come to the realization of the gravity of his little escapade, the two Boston diplomats smoothed things over with the offended Mogulites, and came away feeling that once more they had made their peace-calling and election sure.

Now for the probable sequel. If the understanding was for Barilla to stay with Boston till the Boston bill was through the legislature, he had fulfilled his promise when the bill was sent to the governor.

As stated before, Ex-Senator Barilla is probably the only man living that could give the inside story of that Tioga-Baca affair; but what we were inclined to believe at the time was that it was Barilla with his little hatchet that cut down our cherry tree, and that the abuse heaped upon him by Hughes at Trinidad while celebrating the freedom of the city was the sequel of his shifting the gears when left free to do so.

One thing is certain, Barilla was one of the few who had a seat well up to the front of those belonging to the inside circle, and all he had to do at any time he was wanting the gears to shift was to give the signal.

As to Hughes, whether he came back a broken-hearted man or not we do not know; but we do know he came back to a broke -- and friendless -- town.

He remained in town but a short time, a week or such a matter, and, like all the others afterward, left never to return. He came to Boston reputed to be worth $75,000, and he got away with anything from $1,000 to $6,000.

Hughes we understand went to Washington and into the store business, but whether he is still there and whether he has made good we do not know.

But Boston, the probable one-time county seat of Tioga County, the largest town in all the east end -- all there is now to tell its tragic story are piles of stone and holes in the ground.[166]

That is it close into the banks of the North Fork of the Great American desert, lying midway between the range lines of 43 and 44 and a milepost south of the center of the town lines 32 and 33 -- all somewhere in the north temperate zone of the once wild North American continent.

Should you ever chance to visit the shrine of the defunct city, stop long enough to shed a tear to the tomb of its departed glory and offer up a prayer for the souls of those who were buried beneath its ruins.

It's all over now and has been for the past thirty years, during which the ground has been made hollowed as a range for livestock, coyotes, and badgers while its one-time rollicking, hopeful care-free people have been scattered as were the children of the lost tribes of Israel. Goodbye, poor old Boston, for the present--we'll call again another day.

Goodbye poor ol Boston for the present
will call again another day.[167]

Chapter 16: A Deadly Feud

"Every man goes about armed to the teeth, for village is at war with village, and blood feuds are as abundant as stones on the ground."

-The Winfield Tribune, 1889

Most writings about Boston, agree that the feud between Doc Brown, the merchant, and the cow boys led to the murder of a young cow boy named Newt Bradley. Each version has details which differ, but the basic story is the same. Previous accounts also compress the timetable of when Bradley was killed and how long it took for the final events of Boston to occur. All earlier accounts make it appear Bradley was murdered and within a few days or weeks, the cow boys came to avenge his death. However, Bradley was killed in December of 1887 while the final siege of Boston did not occur until April of 1889. These dates imply it took much longer for the cow boys to return to avenge Bradley than previous accounts have implied.

The one constant in the various versions of this story is Bradley was murdered. The story carried far and wide as the news clippings below attest.[168] [169] [170]

A Dead Desperado.

Philadelphia, Ks., Dec. 17.—News was received here to-day that Newt Bradley, a desperado, was killed at Boston, Colorado, by the town marshal while trying to run the place. Bradley formerly resided here, and was the leader of a bad gang.

It is reported from Richfield, Kansas, that Neut Bradley, a tough and ballot box thief was killed at Boston, Colorado, Thursday.

Richfield, Kas, Dec. 17.—At Boston, Colorado, on Thursday, Newt Bradley, a tough, formerly of this county, was killed by the marshal while trying to do the town. Bradley and his gang of renegades have on several times done this town and attempted to capture a ballot box at the county election last February, but were prevented by an organization of citizens.

The killing of Bradley is the critical event leading up to the final siege of Boston. Besides the loss of the county seat, this event, more than any other, impacted the demise of the town. The basic fact is a drunk Newt Bradley came into Doc Brown's store causing trouble. This confrontation led to Bradley's murder. Doc Brown played a role in the killing, but his part is sketchy. However, he is the person most often blamed for the events of the day. We shall review the stories surrounding this murder before moving on, in the next chapter, to other factors leading to the siege and subsequent demise of Boston.

The Murder of Newt Bradley

J.R. Austin published *"A History of Early Baca County"* in 1936. This book contains the most common version of the Newt Bradley murder. Austin cites no references, but mentions in the text a conversation with Abel Capansky about the events in Boston. Ike Osteen's 1979 version of this event in his book, *"A Place Called Baca,"* appears to be a derivative of the story Austin told in 1936. Ike does add discussion of the murder of John Phillips in the Neutral Strip.

Austin, Osteen and Capansky accounts all use the name Frank Bradley. The Sam Konkel and Alberta Clark versions referred to Bradley as Neut or Newt. All of the newspaper accounts from the time supporting the story also refer to him as Neut or Newt as well. It can be concluded Neut, Newt and Frank all refer to the same person.

J. R. Austin's version is the same as the 1954 Capansky interview provided below with a slight variation in how the incident began and an addition in which he mentions that Bradley, after being shot and leaning against the building murmured "You got me, boys!" Osteen's version is nearly identical to Austin's version.

The events in Austin's 1936 account of the story says, Boston's downfall began when Frank/ Newt walked into a store and ordered some canned food. After setting the cans on a counter, he wanted to eat their contents but lacked a can opener. He drew his revolver and shot the tops of the cans off as patrons were sprayed with the substances and ran for cover.

Abel Capansky who was a boy of 10 years old in Boston when all the events unfolded recounts the story in a July 25, 1954 interview with The Pueblo Star-Journal and Sunday Chieftain..

"Another friend of Thompson's was a cowboy from Texas, Frank Bradley, who was always getting drunk and creating a disturbance. It seems he had always been confident his friendship with the regulator Thompson would save him from any serious trouble. While Thompson and the cow boys were out of town, Bradley went on one of his drunken sprees.

Cornelius Smith, the town marshal, attempted to arrest Bradly, but after being nipped in the ear by a bullet from Bradley's gun, he withdrew. Frank Lepel, went in and grabbed Bradley from behind and dragged him outside. He se-cured Bradley's gun and tossed it into the darkness. A circle of bystanders had gathered, and while Lepel sat on Bradley's chest, an onlooker walked up and pointed a gun at Bradley and shot him. Bradley, staggered to his feet, slumped against a building and died. "[171]

Alberta Clark, was the daughter of J.J. Burnett whose restaurant was south east of Doc Browns store. She is the second of three people who wrote their account of the story. She tells us,

"The incident which led to the shooting up of old Boston was the death of a Cowboy by the name of Newt Bradley. Bradley came into town, got drunk and entering the store of Doc Brown, pulled his gun and let loose at various objects around Brown's place. Drunkenness was not an unusual display in that place and time, but perhaps Doc Brown did not know it was harmless and anyhow did not want his windows shot out. So he sent for the marshall, Lew Reader,[172] *who shot the cowboy, wounding him and took his gun away. Then on the pretense of reviving him, Brown went behind his counter and came out with a dose of poison, which he administered, killing him instantly"*[173]

Sam Konkel's version of the story goes as follows,

Dr. Brown

The doctor has already been extensively noticed in "Fortunes Brought, Made and Lost" but is further here because of his relation to some other particularly interesting things in the history of the good old town.

The most important of these events was the killing of Neut Bradley, on one of the occasions of one of his drunken carousals. Neut Bradley, when on one of these carousals, was one of the most dangerous of the so-called cow boys who sometimes rode into town, and sometimes celebrated their visits by having a hallelujah time at the different bars of the town that became saloons when the country went to the bad and town became depopulated.

We shall here give two instances of the escapades and dangerous nature of this man Bradley.

There was a boy of simple wit whom the boys would often deputize as a constable or sheriff and send out to arrest someone – especially when that someone was calling on his best girl. On this occasion, he was deputized to arrest Neut Bradley when the latter was on one of his drunks, which of course was an unwise, imprudent and dangerous thing for the boys to put him up to.

It was in Doc Brown's store, and when the boy advanced to put Bradley under arrest, the latter poked him in the ribs with his cocked gun a few times, and then grabbed his hat off his head, threw it down at his (the boy's) feet and shot it full of holes.

At another time Bradley was taking out a part of his drunken celebration in the Boston Grocery, when Judge Jennings chanced to enter the front door.

Bradley for some minutes had been keeping a few persons in the store guessing, and when the judge entered he turned his attention to said judge, and in a maudlin friendly way began to badger him.

Shoving his cocked gun against the Judge's breast said – "I've got a notion to shoot you there." Then pointing it towards his head said – "I've got a notion to shoot you there" Then, point the gun accordingly, said – no I believe I will shoot that ink bottle" (on the showcase): and smash went the bottle and the showcase.

When Bradley was in his "oh-be-joyful" moods it was up to Billy the Kid – city marshal, to disarm him; and when he needed help he would deputize someone to assist him. For some reason, Doc Brown has a special fear of Bradley, and entertained a suspicion that some of the so-called cow boys for some reason had it in for him.

On the night of the killing Bradley seems to have been on the hunt for Doc Brown, at least Doc thought so, and Bradley was so reckless that Billy deputized Frank Lepel – a brother of our worthy old timer of Boston,[174] to help disarm him.

During the scuffle, several shots were fired by the delirious Bradley before his gun could be taken away from him, but they finally got it and then he crossed over the street and started to return when there was another shot fired.

The writer came upon the scene as Bradley was laying on the counter and Doc was giving him some medicine – in his store. We are not certain whether he died on the counter or not, but at least he died that night – without regaining consciousness.

The first report was that Frank Lepel had shot Bradley in the tussle to disarm him, but at the inquest the fact came out that the shot had been fired after the man had been disarmed and had crossed over the street, and finally – after some weeks, the cow boys came to understand, or at least believe, that it was Doc Brown that fired the solitary shot that put out Bradley's light.

"Ten Nights in a Bar Room," the cow boy alarm, the hunt for a girl and Docs escape from the town—next week.[175]

Chapter 17: Coming of the Cow boys

**"An elderly gentleman on his way to Colorado was asked
what there was attractive there, and answered 'Nothing sir,
but a dry burying ground and shorter route to Heaven"**

-The Ashland Weekly Journal, 1887

The first event leading up to the siege was the killing of Newt.
Bradley. The second event leading up to the siege was an editorial in
the *Boston Banner*, by George Daniel, and the third event was the humiliation of the Jennings protégé, Lou Reeder by the Cow boys. Sam
Konkel lists these two events in addition to the feud between Doc
Brown as the reasons for the Cow boys coming back to Boston. Following the murder of Henry Savoy, George Daniel of the Boston
Banner wrote a scathing editorial about the regulator Big Bill Thompson. Sam Konkel says of the editorial,

"In his paper, *The Banner*, Geo Daniel called Bill
Thompson a cold-blooded murderer, and otherwise
berated and lampooned him ⸗ as a low-browed
ingrate, highway ruffian, etc. in a lengthy editorial.
Neither Daniel or anyone else thought that Bill would
ever come back to Boston"[176]

However, Thompson did return to Boston. He returned with his
mind on vengence and plenty of help in an attempt to settle the score

with Doc Brown for what he felt like was the murder of Newt Bradley and for the words Daniel wrote in the Boston Banner. The following report is typical of the language describing these events leading to the final siege of the town.[177]

The stage which arrived this evening from Bostontown brings the report that Bill Thompson and his gang left last evening. They had occupied the town since Monday night and completely disarmed the inhabitants. Only one building was fired and this the robbers were induced to extinguish before much damage had been done. The object of the raid was the capture of Dr. Brown and Editor Daniels, but in this they were not successful, as these gentlemen were not to be found. They took during their stay such articles as they needed from stores, but no general pillrge took place. Bill Thompson has an old grudge against Brown and Daniels and swears he will kill them on sight.

The final contributing factor was the humiliation of Lou Reeder. Konkel goes into much detail on each of these issues later.

Sam Konkel describes the final days of Boston as follows,

The Final Grand Round-Up

Contributing Causes

The killing of Henry Savoy by Bill Thompson was probably the first incident leading up to the final round-up.

Those of our readers who have been following up these old time writings, will remember the Thompson-Savoy shooting.

Neither Daniel nor anyone else thought that Bill would ever come back to Boston. But Bill came back -- He and others from the neutral strip -- the day before the play *10 nights in a Bar Room.*

Of course there was a nervous tension. Daniel was in the play, and it being feared that an attempt will be made to pick him off the stage while the play was in progress, firearms were stored under the stage for instant use, while one citizen without being suspected, stood right by the side of old Bill until the performance was over and the coast was clear.

The killing of Newt Bradley was another contributing cause. We have already told of the relation of Doc Brown to this killing, of the hunt for the doctor afterward by the cow boys, and of his being hauled out of town under a load of fodder with some dry good boxes piled on top.

The third indirect contributing cause was the kicking of Lou Reeder out of the saloon just the night before the grand ball was to be open.

The two factors of the hostile move that brought on the battle in the succeeding roundup, caused by the incidents related, were in the first place, fear and in the second place, a desire for revenge.

On the part of Doc and Daniel it was presumably a mixture of both. Doc particularly was in a nervous tension, as he knew that the killing of Newt Bradley was still rankling in the breast of old Bill -- Bradley's foster father; and George knew that old Bill was still chafing over the fiery attack made on him by George in his paper.

The Coming of the Cow boys

We will here leave these contributing causes, for the direct events that led to the never to be forgotten round up of the town.

On Tuesday April 9th, in the year of our Lord 1889, it being year 1 in the organization of Baca County, by which the doom of the great Boston hub city had already been sealed. Bill Thompson, Bill Rowan and Ed Maxwell and five other so-called cow boys from the neutral strip, rode into town armed with Winchester s and other belligerent weapons of offense and defense according as the necessity of the occasion might require.

A Request

When you have read the old time story of this issue, hand your copy (unless you re a filing them as some are doing), to your neighbor and tell him these old-time write-ups will continue during the year 1919, and that five new Baca County maps at the present time are given with the Herald at the regular subscription price at $1.50.

The great Roundup story will itself be carried to several issues of the paper, and when it is over something else will follow, just as one blooming thing always follows another.[178]

Doc Brown Continued

With the knowledge, or belief, that Doc Brown had fired the solitary shots and that it was this shot that killed Bradley, his so-called cow boy friends become very sullen, and the feelings of the whole town against them were of a sullen nature.

The leader of the cow boys was one Bill Thompson. Second to Bill Thompson in his relations with Boston and the settlement was Bill Rowan, who was also domiciled in the outlaw country.

The interesting thing of Bill Thompson in connection with the killing was that he was Bradley's foster father, having raised him from boyhood up – presumedly in the "No Man's Land" country.

At the time the tension between Boston and the cow boys, over the killing of Bradley, was close to the breaking point, word was received that the cow boys were coming up in force to avenge their illustrious comrade's death, the occasion of the calling being timed with the giving of the entertainment by Boston Amateurs of

"Ten Nights in a Bar Room"

According to the announcement the cow boys were on hand that day – five of them riding in with Winchesters, besides the usual equipment of the hip-pocket paraphernalia.

A Boston Colorado amateur dramatic troup is going to play "Ten Nights in a Bar Room" on New Year's eve. The people of Kansas can now realize the full extent of a prohibitory liquor law. We escape a'l that, for we don't enjoy such luxuries you know.

Syracuse Kansas news of the upcoming Boston Play "Ten Nights in a Bar Room"[179]

To aggravate the case and add to its uncertainty, W. H. Yaw had in his livery barn some horses that the cow boys claimed he got down in the No Mans Land illegally; and when they came into town they went to the barn and got the horses. No one ever knew the particulars, but apparently, Yaw's title to the horses was not at least very strong. After getting the horses two of the boys rode away with them the others remaining.

Another matter that added to the fear and uncertainty – Geo. Daniel, on the occasion of the killing of Savoy by Thompson, thought Thompson would never come back again and grilled him in his paper as a desperado and a murderer.

As George was in the play and it was feared that the cow boys might make some break in the entertainment, certain armed parties were delegated to be at the side of the cow boys in the audience, while under the stage was stored a whole armament of trusty repeating rifles that were come-at-able on a moments notice.

The play was rendered without molestation, however, and the night passed off quietly; but the tension was not lessened and the uncertainty remained as before.

The next couple of days though were strenuous ones for our illustrious Dr. Brown, who as the vengeance traffickers came into the front of his store, made the exit out the back door, and hid himself in the cellar under the residence part of Burnett's grocery and bakery.

The cellar had been used for the storage of garbage, boxes, waste paper, rags, etc and of course the musty, rusty and dusty.

It being, as Doc believed, a case of emergency, he laid himself down in a musty corner of the cellar, while Mr. Burnett piled boxes, rags and all kinds of rubbish over and around him to protect him against inquisitive cow boy eyes.

All forenoon they had searched Boston over for Doc Brown but without results.

It was probably half afternoon when they entered the Burnett Bakery at the front.

To get from the store to the living room, a door opened into a side hall and another door from the side hall into the living room – the hall also opening into the cellar, just a trifle further on from the door into the living room.

Not knowing they were around Miss Alice Burnett stepped through the door to the living room into the hall as the cow boys were walking down the hall from the other door, and realizing their probable purpose of entering the cellar gave a scream and ⸗Fell into a faint to the floor.

Mr. and Mrs. Burnett ran out and took charge of Alice, while Bill Thompson expressed his regret at having scared the girl, declared they wouldn't harm a hair of any of their heads, and said they would go away at once and not further bother them.

Whether they were headed for the cellar or not was not known, but they probably were, and if they were it is probable the fainting of the girl saved the doctor's life – or at least his hide and probably some of his bones.

It was probably an hour before sundown when a team with some fodder in the wagon bed drove up to the east side of the residence part of the store.

Thereupon Doc came out from under the rubbish, squeezed his way through the cellar window, crawled into the end of the wagon, was covered carefully over with fodder, with some boxes and was thus. **Hauled out of town.**

The man who drove up with the wagon and hauled the badley frightened doctor out of town was the writer's brother and the place of refuge was our home.

Something else next week. [180]

The Burnetts hung on a little longer than most, as this ad from the Baca County Journal in 1890, almost a year after the final siege attests. [181]

SHOT BY THOMPSON'S GANG.

Editor Daniels, of Boston, Col., Hounded by Toughs.

BLOODTHIRSTY DESPERADOES.

Pueblo (Col.) special: The gang of desperadoes who took possession of Boston, this state, last Friday and Saturday, with the object of killing Dr. Brown and Editor Daniels, who were not to be found, however, rushed down upon the town last night, surrounded Editor Daniels' residence, and opened fire. Daniels ran out the back door and started to escape, but was pierced by two bullets and fell to the ground. The robbers supposing that they had finished Daniels rode to the residence of Dr. Brown and commenced firing, but the doctor by this time had got wind of the raid and made good his escape. The robbers, after running the town for a few hours and stealing such articles as they desired to carry away, left for the neutral strip, where the officers of this county seat have no authority to arrest, and which is very dangerous of approach. Active measures will now be taken by the state authorities to break up this, the most desperate gang of outlaws that inhabit Colorado. Daniels will probably die. He was shot in the right side and the hip.

Konkel doesn't mention George Daniel getting shot but there are several reports similar to the one above.[182]

The Final Grand Round-Up

The Commotion

The coming of the eight cow boys, with Winchesters, and other-wise armed to the teeth, at a time when the strain was at the breaking point, caused an undercurrent of excitement and apprehension that had never previously per-turbed the calm feeling of the town.

Had the public known what probably a half dozen cit-izens knew, there would have been less cause of apprehension, and probably no excitement at all.

But the public had nothing but a surmise as to what they had come for, and as near as they could surmise that coming was to round-up and get revenge on certain ones in the town, with the possibility that the whole town might fall a victim to that revenge.

The first move they made was to compel Tom O'Neal and a Mr. Vandyke to give up a horse they claimed the boys took from a pasture in the strip from of one of them.

We never learned what explanation the boys made of the matter -- apparently because they had none to make. The town was somewhat stunned by the dubious nature of the case, as Tom particularly was presumed to be straight as a string -- when pulled tight.

The next move of the cow boys was both stunning and confounding. They went to the barn of W. H. Yaw, presumed to be one of our most reputable citizens, and abstracted from there five horses that Yaw apparently didn't have a quieting title to.

Yaw had been down in the strip sometimes previous, and came back with quite a bunch of horses -- may be a dozen or more.

After the boys had taken the five out of the barn, Yaw had very little to say as to how he got them, thus leaving the citizens in a state of bewilderment as to the actual facts of the case.

All this took place on Tuesday. The work was done in rapid order, and as soon as done five of the cow boys started with the horses on the return to the strip, Bill Thompson, Ed Maxwell and Bill Rowan remaining.

An incident in the saloon that night we believe was directly responsible for what took place the next night -- anyway was a big factor in it.

It was in the neighborhood of 10 o'clock. The three cow boys, Lou Reeder and some of the others were in the saloon.

Impelled by a desire to show his recklessness and dare devilism, Lou stood back of the stove twirling his shining six on his finger at arm s length.

Ed Maxwell told him "_____ your soul, put up that gun."

To this Lou replied "____your soul, go to h___" and kept on twirling the gun.

The next thing he knew Maxwell had him by the shoulders, marched him to the door, applied the toe of his boot to where he thought it would do the most good, and with that, and a very vigorous shove, sent him out on the side- walk -- of course in a foaming rage.

Ditto next time.[183]

The Final Grand Round-Up

The Conspiracy

The final factor leading up the Grand Roundup was an event in which Lou Reeder was embarrassed by the cow boys. His loss of prestige for bravery and as a bad man to fool with, by being kicked out of the saloon with the shin- ing bulldozer in his hand, called for revenge to even things up a little.

We think it probable that Lou Reeder was the princi- pal instigator in the organization of a citizen battalion whose purpose it was to wipe the so-called cow boy band off the face of the earth.

The Conspiracy

It was the next day after the kicking of Reeder out of the saloon. Lou, Doc Brown and Geo. Daniel and about seventeen other Bostonians, organized themselves into a vig- ilante committee, the intent and purpose of which was to have less cow boys on the face of the earth, and thus to make the country safer for the rest of mankind.

For this purpose, they provided themselves with shot guns and repeating rifles, and presumably about forty rounds of ammunition to the head to feed the guns.

The saloon that Lou had been kicked out of was on the southeast corner of the Main Street and 9th avenue, while at the center of the crossing of these two streets was the famous Boston public well.

At this public well had been erected a large water tank, something like twenty feet long and probably four feet high, made out of two inch plank. Our recollection is that it sat diagonally across the street, northeast to southwest.

Diagonally across the street from the saloon was the Wright grocery store -- northeast corner of the block butting up to the two aforesaid streets.

The Fusillade

The Western World office was a block west of the saloon mentioned, on 9th avenue.

It was probably 10:30 or later that the writer closed his office and ambled towards his earthly habitation for nightly repose. With comfort under one arm to give aid in giving a little more protection against the old boreas.

We were hibernating in the palatial abode of a dugout, with two other bipeds, about one block north from the saloon, going and coming at right and left angles

We were probably half way from the office to the burrowed out sleeping quarters, when there was suddenly a discharge of musketry or riflery in the direction of the sa-loon causing us to stop and wonder.

After the first fusillade there was a moment's stillness, and then the popping of the guns was mingled with yells and curses, not quite equal to the concussions of the atmos-phere in an artillery duel.

We walked on up to the dugout and threw the comfort down on the storm door.

Was the fears of the citizens being realized, and was the town being shot up by the cow boys?

That was the thought of everyone not inside the citizen conspiracy-- and in the mind of the writer.

With nothing but a pocket knife and too dull to whittle with, there wasn't much the writer could do to protect the old town in case the cow boys were actually seeking out their vengeance on it.

But we might reconnoiter, so we turned back towards the office for that purpose. Back of the office and extending to the alley was a high and tight board fence, for what purpose we could not now tell. As this board fence would take us within good hearing distance, we walked along the north side of it to the alley, and then listened for some time in an effort to analyze the trouble.

We weren't near enough to get an exact line up on the nature of the talk, but finally made up our mind that the cow boys were simply shooting up the saloon and that wasn't any of our hog killing so we turned around and went back along the side of the fence until opposite the office, when we again struck across the lot for that "home, sweet home" in the dugout.[184]

The Final Boston Grand Round-Up

We were probably halfway on our journey to that " home sweet home" in The Dugout, when a clarion voice in the directions to saloon rang out clear and distinct on the stillness of the air -- "There goes one of them now." This being followed by the crack of a gun.

Having decided that the cow boys were simply shooting up the saloon, of course, this outcry, followed by the crack of a gun, didn t at that time carry with them any direct significance.

We stopped and listened for a moment and then ambled onto the dugout. Reaching it, we pick up the comfort we had dropped down on the storm door and attempting open the door, found to our surprised that it was hooked on the inside.

That was a puzzle. We never fasten the doors from any side, and took in from the outside on the inside -- that was sure one on us.

We gave it a second slight pull to make sure, and then in an undertone exclaimed -- "well I ll be hanged!"

And then a trembling and scared voice from the inside exclaimed outwardly -- "who's there?"

"Why it's me," The writer ungrammatically explained. "What have you got the door fastened for?"

Then the hook was unhooked and the voice inside said

"Come in quick and latch the door."

"What in blazes is the matter with you?" the writer asked as he stepped inside.

We saw at once that our partners in crime-- meaning our roommates, were greatly excited. They immediately plied us with questions to get an understanding of what was going on the outside, and their excitement added another feature to the puzzle of the situation.

We explained to them that the cow boys were simply shooting up the saloon, and there was nothing to get excited about; but they implored us in turning the light off at once, so that wouldn t betray our whereabouts-- " as one couldn t tell what might happen."

Here it becomes necessary to explain who these two roommates were.

The one was Dr. McCrory, whom we have mentioned a few times. Doc had no direct relationship with the roundup in anyway, so isn t here of direct importance.

Geo Nethercut was the other roommate. We have also mentioned him before. George set in on the games and won and lost money-- as do all gamblers.

The one thing we didn t know at this time that would have served as a sequel to the twain agitation was that Geo. Nethercut and Bill Lindley at one time went down to the neutral strip, and representing themselves as U.S. Marshals, brought back a couple of horses they bluffed as one of the worshippers of Baal down there into giving up.

We are just presuming that they went on the theory that those fellows in the strip stole everything they had anyway, and hence by the U.S. Marshal racket they could round up some of the stolen stuff and nothing would ever be done about it. The rest of the part of the story will explain itself further on.

Ditto Next Week[185]

Chapter 18: Siege of Boston

"Boston, Las Animas County was terrorized last week by a band of desperados who took the town by violence, shot the buildings full of holes, ransacked everything they wanted, insulted women and did everything that was fiendish. Quiet has at last been restored."

-*The Walsenburg World,* 1889

The story of the siege of Boston was carried in newspapers coast to coast with a couple samples of story show as follows. Note the error. The report mentions Trill Thompson, which is actually Big Bill Thompson being an associate of Billy the Kid.[186]

The Town of Boston, Colorado, in Possession of a Gang of Outlaws.

COLORADO FREEBOOTERS.

LAMAR, COL., April 13.—Boston, a town eighty-five miles south of here, and the same distance from any railroad, is in possession of a gang of outlaws headed by Trill Thompson, an old pal of "Billy the Kid." They have taken possession of stores, saloons and the postoffice, and have demanded the contents, and threaten the lives of citizens if they attempt any interference. The town has been fired in several places, and the people have fled to the surrounding country for safety. It is feared that the town will be burned.

A Bad Outfit.

The Thompson gang of horse thieves that has caused so much trouble south of here, is in a fair way to be rounded up, and in case they are captured by the indignant settlers they will no doubt receive the punishment they so much merit and what that will be is not difficult for a person who has spent years on the frontier to surmise. A few days ago the gang made a raid on Boston, Colo., and Thompson was shot in the breast by a Winchester ball. Unfortunately he was protected by a heavy steal shield which prevented the ball from knocking a lung or two out of his worthless carcass. As was he was knocked from his horse, but succeeded in remounting and making off before another bullet could be placed where it would have done more good. It is reported that his outfit contemplated holding up one of the Ft. Worth trains but desisted when it was discovered that there was several Texas rangers aboard.—*Coolidge Citizen.* Old settlers say that the Thompson above referred to conducted a horse ranch north of here some years ago. Rumor also has it that he has gathered around him several parties well known here and that they constitute the gang.

Typical article describing the siege of Boston.[187]

Sam Konkel describes the events beginning April 9, 1889 as follows.

The Final Boston Grand Round-Up

What Actually Happened

We have given the Roundup story so far as seen and heard by those on the outside of the doings-- and so far as they knew about it at the time.

We have told of the citizen vigilante organization. We do not know the exact number that was banded together, but generally was considered to be about twenty, and twenty we should consider it for the present purposes.

Vigilantes, as already stated had provided themselves with such artillery and munitions as they thought the oc-casion would call for and presumedly in the neighborhood of 9 or 10 p.m. filed out in a line behind that old city well tank and then awaited their opportunity.

We never did learn, but presume they had regularly ordained generals, Colonels, Captain s, Etc. and probably had regular drill parades, though we actually presume to the contrary.

It is said that all things which of course includes opportunity comes to him who waits.

We don t know how long those boys waited behind that public tank barricade, but one third of the opportunity for which they were waiting finally popped over that tank at them, and they acted on the principle that it would be better to take a chance at 1/3 of an opportunity then to let the whole opportunity get away.

The third of an opportunity that presented itself was when Ed Maxwell-- one-third of the Cow boys the citizen vigilantes were laying for, came out of the front door of the saloon and leaned against the banister post thereof-- to kinder get a breath of fresh air.

"Bang! Bang!! Bang! Bang! Bang! Bang! Bang! Bang! Bang! Bang! Bang!"

It was the guess of the citizen soldier army ambuscaded in all the trenches behind that public pig trough that were speaking.

Apparently, the generalissimo of the citizen army didn t have the sufficient discipline or one third of an opportunity was thought by some of them too good to let pass, so when Maxwell leaned against the awning post, one gun turned loose, and then two or three - and then something like a half a dozen, and then all of them in one grand discharge.

At the first crack of a gun Maxwell dropped to the sidewalk and crawled through the door and the inside -- as if old Nick were after him.

At the time the salutatory guns were fired, there were in the saloon the saloon keepers -- Cox and son, and Ed Jennings, Jno. McCoach and a Mr. Bush (that is in addition to the three cow boys).

The three later were standing at the bar-- in exact range of the guns, when the hail opened and probably only the glass front served to deflect the bullets, and save their lives. As it was they were splattered with glass and the plate mirror back of the bar was shattered into pieces.

Maxwell probably dropped to the sidewalk just in time to beat the coroner out of a fee and the undertaker out of a job but enough not quite in time to save his necktie, as it was carried away in the first fusillade. The post against what he was leaning showed the scars of several buckshot, So long as it continued to be a post.

As soon as Maxwell could get himself inside of the hole the carpenters left in front of the saloon, the hole was closed and the three said cow boys grab their guns and made a bolt for the rear side door and looked cautiously out, the intention being to make their everlasting getaway-- while the getting was good.

But when they got to the door and peered through the moon lightness in the direction of the public well, they saw the hosts of Moab doing just what they were intending to do-- hitting the high places in the direction of taller timber.

That view of the situation gave them an inspiration, and quick as a flash they dropped down on their middle extremities and got those Winchesters to the shoulders and with curses and yells begin to pump lead in the direction of those "Christian Soldiers" who were going onward in the other direction.

Ditto next time[188]

The Final Boston Grand Round-Up

Actual Happenings

We are presuming that those hosts of Moab, individually and collectively, jumped about four feet high when
those Philistine guns begin to pop and that they couldn t
hit mor'n about one percent of the high places in their
frenzy flight for freedom, and to beat the game warden
out of the Happy Hunting-grounds out of some new homesteaders and locating fees.

Presumably, those hosts of Moab had gotten about all
the homestead experience they were wanting -- in a country, they knew nothing about; so as was the first
inspiration of the naughty Philistines, they thought it a
good idea to make their everlasting getaway-- while the
getting was good.

Presumably, also the Generalissimo and the under generals in the officers of the Armageddon Army tried to save
the situation in the cause by calling on their panic-stricken
soldiers to -- "Stand! The ground is your own my braves!"
etc.: though it s barely possible they may have led the
way of the braves to prevent a possible ambush, and that s
to spare their soldiers from the sad fate of the brave Braddock -- when he wouldn t listen to the good advice of an
under officer.

Anyway, the entire army hiked -- officers and privates
alike and so far as anyone knows, they are hiking on to

this day, as there is no record of their ever returning to learn the fate of those cow boy Philistines aforesaid.

It was after the Armageddon Army was scattered and gone that the writer was ambling across to his "home sweet home" in the dugout. This is when the clarion voice sang out -- "There goes one of them now!" the clarion voice being followed by the crack of a gun.

The clarion voice was the voice of the saloon keeper Cox -- who after the Israelites had fled came out of the saloon to help the cow boy Philistines clean things up, and espying the night wanderer, supposed likely to be the last of the Israelites band, called out and ecstasy of his discovery that-- "there goes one of them now," and took a crack at the unsuspecting figure vignetted on the northwestern sky-line.

We are presuming that if the night wanderer had known the last shot of the citizen cow boy war was being aimed at him and was coming in his direction, he would have made the same kind of jump as the citizen soldiers at that the first crack of the Philistine batteries.

And why shouldn t he? General Grant said he was scared to death, shook like an aspen leaf in his knees when the guns begin to pop in the first battle he was in. So why shouldn t the writer along with the citizen soldiers jump when the guns begin to pop in his direction.

But this was an actual case of where "ignorance is bliss." The writer didn t have the least suspicion that the eyes back of that voice were focused on him, and that the gun giving out the "bang!" was pointing in the same direction.

Hence after stopping for a second at the crack of the gun, he ambled on unconcernedly and leisurely to his earthly habitation for nightly repose, just as if that little serenading party over at the saloon were a prayer meeting instead of a running battle.

Ditto next time[189]

The Final Boston Grand Round-Up

Actual Happenings

After there weren t any longer anything for them to shoot at, the three cow boy soldiers went over to the Wright Grocery Store, angling across from the saloon, piled dry good boxes up against the north side of it and set them afire, and returned to the saloon to see them burn-- The why of burning down Wright's store was that Wright was known be one of the Armageddon soldiers.

Capt. McCoach had done his part cussing the Citizen s Army, particularly as it was breaking in on his efforts at collecting the $25 attorney fee from old Bill Thompson previously mentioned; but when the roaring blaze of the dry goods boxes were lapping the north side of the store - - that was more than Mac could stand, so he exclaimed --

"Bill, for God's sake don t burn the town. These people that are here now are not in with that outlaw band, they had nothing to do with it and they re innocent. For God's sake don t burn the town ⁓ take it out of the fellows that were in on the shooting."

The plea had its effect in reaching old Bill's better nature, so he exclaimed, ⁓ "John, if you say so, I ll go over there and kick those boxes away;" and in the glare of that now roaring bonfire Bill Thompson went over there and kick the boxes away from the building, taking the chance of being picked off in that practically daylight ex⁓ pose, by possible citizen⁓soldiers hiding nearby behind sidewalks or buildings.

Probably five or ten minutes more and kicking those boxes away would have been too late, as part of the build⁓ ing was charred by the intense blaze, and soon itself would have been a mass of flames.

Sometime during the night, after the cow boys had gotten themselves indoors and all was "quiet on the Poto⁓ mac." Two or three of the citizen soldiers slipped back to some place in town where they would be safe, one of them particularly will be mentioned later on.

It was a night of the 10th day of April, and the night was cold⁓ not stormy, but raw as ordinarily is the case that time of the year.

Notwithstanding, all but two or three lay down on the prairie till towards morning and then hit the high places for other climes, or walked the whole night through in their effort to get out of harm s way.

Anyway, not one of those who walked the night through, or slept out on the prairie, ever again returned to the town, and as stated before, so far as we know, or anybody but themselves knows, they may be hiking to this day.

The cow boys themselves, and Capt. McCoach and Ed Jennings along after midnight when everything had quieted down-- when "nothing was stirring, not even a mouse," bivouacked on the floor of that saloon, along with the saloon keepers, and slept till morning -- only one of them standing guard to prevent a possible afternight rush on them by the citizens band, and they should just go the way of that Woodsdale, Kansas seven boys who lost their lives at the haystack in Oklahoma -- because they failed to have such a guard.

Ditto next time[190]

The Final Boston Grand Round-Up

Actual Happenings

And the night passed and the morning dawned -- just as nights and mornings have come and gone since the world can remember.

All unconscious of the whys and wherefores of the night's happenings and with very little understanding of the happenings themselves, in the early morning after, the writer, coming down the sidewalk on the west side of Main street and still wearing that campaign plug hat, met Bill Thompson a short ways north of the saloon --

"Just see here what the citizens did last night," said he and he led the way to the front of the saloon, where a little to our surprise we found the glass front of the saloon scattered everywhere in all kinds of little and big pieces.

"They were hid right over there behind that watering tank," he continued, "and fired in on us."

"Well I'll be eternally hanged," we replied: They surely did a good job of it and we went on to the hotel wondering what ol' Bill took for a vigilante.

At the hotel, we got our first inkling of the actual night's events, and of that citizen soldier band, and then understood that old Bill wasn't giving us any moonshine when he told us of that citizen band behind the watering tank.

The day crowded itself thick with events, piled one on another. In the very first place, Ed Maxwell and Bill

Rowan rounded up the town for guns, presumedly getting every gun.

Incidentally, we haven't any idea of how many guns they got, or what they did with them after they got them. We are not presuming though that there were many after the citizen soldiers hiked out with what they had, and think it likely they threw what they did get into some of the city wells.

The cow boys showed no disposition to round up or trouble those who were not connected with the Israelitish soldiers or who had not previously formed any "entangling alliances" down in the outlawed country of "No Man's Land"

Hence the writer ambled about over town, surmounted with that aforesaid silk plug hat, which is supposed to be a standing target for outlaws to shoot at, without previous warning or further provocation ⁓ not questions asked or privileges taken.

It was probably 9:00 or 10:00 a.m. when the first lively and eye-opening event of the morning took place.

The event was ⁓ Ed Maxwell riding a horse by the side of the sidewalk, with his Winchester across his saddle, and big Bill Lindley on the sidewalk, something over a block north of the saloon, towards which both were going. The gun on the saddle was pointing straight at big Bill Lindley, and Ed Maxwell said –

"You'll be a United States Marshal, will you, you ____ ___ a ____! You'll be a United States marshal, will you!"

And Bill was saying ·· "I fixed that with Bill Rowan yesterday, I fixed it with Rowan."

But Maxwell wasn't hearing anything Lindley was saying and kept right on cussing him··

I ought to knock your ____ ____ head off you·you ____ ____ a ____ etc. etc. from the time he first started Bill Lindley from his home down the sidewalk, until he landed him in the saloon and turned him over to Bill Thompson for safe keeping.

Ditto next Week[191]

The Final Boston Grand Round-Up

Actual Happenings

When the twain had reached the saloon Lindley stood at attention while Maxwell tied his horse and then marched in front of that ugly Winchester to a chair in the middle of the room and sat down, according to orders, while Maxwell kept right on cussing him.

In a short time, Bill Thompson came in, and Maxwell turned the prisoner over to him and went on out looking for more worlds to conquer.

"Bill, I made that all right with Rowan yesterday, and if I could see him I know it would be all right."

"We'll see about that when Rowan comes in", said Bill "and you can just sit where you are till he comes."

Ed Maxwell dropped back in a couple times before Bill Rowan came in, and every time would cuss Bill Lindley for all of them were worth.

He returned for the third time and was walking down the saloon towards Lindley when Rowan met him and explained --

"That's all right, Ed, Lindley fixed that all right yesterday." Then Maxwell went on up to Lindley and said -

"___ ___ your old soul, I ought to break your head for you anyway.

Now you get up and get out of here, and don't you let me catch you out on the streets again, you _____, get out!"

It was probably an hour later when the writer coming into that saloon observed Jack Fisher sitting in that same chair, which now might be called "the prisoner's chair."

Jack is the fellow you will remember, that Lou Reeder rooted away from the arm connections with the widow, taking the widow unto himself and on to her home.

But that little episode was like a Sunday school picnic by the side of the matinee that was being pulled off that fateful day in the old town of Boston, in which Jack was one of the principal figures

Jack always had a pleasant look and a bright smile on his face when meeting anyone, but the prisoner s chair took all that bright smile out of him and left his face as white as a corpse.

"Jack," said the writer when opportunity offered, "I'm very sorry for you, and wish I could help you."

"I'll be all right," said Jack, "and thank you just the same."

Truly, if any mortal had our sympathy it was Jack Fisher, as he sat in that prisoner s chair, with a look on his face that showed there wasn't a glimmer of hope.

We will leave Jack temporarily now while we tell of the dragnet in which he was caught, and the circumstances under which he and others were forced to surrender.

We have told of some of those citizen soldiers returning in the still hours of the night to some place of safety in the town, one of whom we said we would notice later on.

Jack Fisher was that one. He was with the citizen army, and after the cow boys had turned down the lights and turned in for the night he slipped back to town and into the dugout with two other boys, and there awaited the doom of the coming day, and the fate that was in store for him.

It was probably 10 a.m. when the two cow boys, Ed Maxwell and Bill Rowan, came into the Deputy Drug Store and ordered Deputy to march before them to a certain dug-out about a half a block north of the store.

Deputy had a short leg, walked on a patent shoe, and hence with the usual up and down limp of those with short legs and wearing the patent shoe.

As Deputy was marching in front of the two general-issimos of the Philistine army down to the store, Gene Whitaker came in at the front door and exclaimed--

"Hello, Depy, where you going?" "We'll take you along, also." said Maxwell. "Just move along in front of us with Deputy."

We haven't heard whether our former efficient register of the land office was for or against the draft in the great world war, but on this particular occasion he certainly would have been in favor of "self determination of the peoples," as in being against the draft that was going to put him up to stop the bullets of those boys in the dugout.[192]

The Final Boston Grand Round-Up

Actual Happenings

We are not advised as to how the two prisoners moved forward, whether in a single file or double file; but the bad men constituting the rear guard were in the double file, and the whole procession moved north to visit those boys in the dugout.

When they got to the dugout one of the prisoners knocked on the door and said to the boys on the inside—

"Boys, it's us -- don't shoot -- it's us."

And the boys said -- "What are you doing out there?"

"We two are prisoners--held as hostages -- so don't shoot."

"Tell them to open the door, and that you fellows will kick it in if they don't," said Maxwell as he flourished his peacemaker in close proximity to the halo about the dome of one of the hostages.

"You'd better open the door, boys; they've got us in front of them, and we don't help ourselves."

"What you come over here for anyhow?" Asked one of the boys on the inside.

"Boys, we couldn't help ourselves -- they made us some. Don't you think you'd better open the door?"

Thus each side hedged for time, and then, in the end, the door was opened, and the boys filed out, under the cover of the barkers of the two generalissimos.

Jack Fisher was the one they were after, relieving both host and guest of their shooting irons, all the others were given their liberty, while Jack was marched to the saloon, where the writer found him not long afterward.

They held Jack til about 3 or 4 p.m., trying to make him tell who else was in on the shooting bee the night before.

"I was in it," Jack would say, "but I won't tell who else were in it;" and that was all they could get out of Jack.

"You'll tell who else were in it or you'll go under sod," said Maxwell with the usual Maxwell accompaniment of oaths.

But Jack stood pat, and neither cajolery nor threats could move him to betray those that were in the shooting.

"I was in it," and "I won't tell," was all they could move him to say.

About 3 or 4 p.m. Maxwell came in and said --

"Jack ___ ___ you, you are going to tell me who was in that shooting, you're going to do it now. Get on your hat and we'll go someplace."

And Jack was marched by Ed Maxwell and Bill Rowan to what he supposed was the finis of his career.

As they moved out of town eastward, Maxwell and Rowan told him that they wouldn't kill him if he would tell, but Jack replied simply --

"You can kill me but I won't tell."

Jack knew he was in a band of killers, but nothing could move him to betray his colleagues.

They were half a mile east of town when the procession stopped and Jack was given his last chance to talk.

"You've got your last chance," said Rowan, "You talk right now!" as "click" "click" went the two revolvers.

"I won't tell," said Jack as all the years of his past life rushed before him -- "you can kill me but I won't tell"

Maxwell was the one that acted. He cracked Jack's head a few times with his gun, and then grabbed him by the shoulders, whirled him eastwardly, and said --

"Jack your nose is pointing east. You follow your nose, and don't look back, and don't you ever be caught in this part of the world again."

And with this he gave Jack a shove and a swift kick in the pants, and Jack took them at their word and followed his nose, never once turning his head to the right or to the left, but followed his nose straight to the east, at least till he was out of sight of those man killing Philistines.

Next week again[193]

The Final Boston Grand Round-Up

Actual Happenings

With the departure of Jack Fisher for worlds un-known -- even to himself, the events of the fitful day of Boston s Grand Roundup were about closed and the finis bout written to this exciting chapter of the town s history.

There are only a few other incidents of the day worth relating, and they mostly trivial.

Shortly after Whitaker and Deputy had been paroled on their good behavior, Ed Maxwell and Bill Thompson met Lou Matthews coming into town, when Maxwell wanted to know -- "what in ___ do you want here And who in the_____ are you?"

"Why this is my trading place." replied Lou. "I live right down here."

"I know him," said Thompson-- "he s alright -- come on."

And thus was spoiled what might have been a good story of how Lou Mathews was captured at the point of the bristling bayonet of the daredevil Maxwell, was marched up Main Street to that now historic saloon, sat down in its historic prisoners chair, and afterwards giving his choice to become a great outlaw, as did the Jennings boys afterwards, or a following that great citizen army to worlds un-known -- etcetera and so forth.

Of course at that time Lou was awful glad to get off so easy -- and notwithstanding the spoiling of a good story.

Another trivial incident was that there was one gun those rounders up didn t get. About 10 a.m. one of the younger Konkel boys drove into town and up to the Western World office, and came in and said--

"We've got a gun under some straw in the wagon and plenty of ammunition. "You'd better come get it."

We brought the gun and hid it. We didn t believe that we would be compelled to use it but of course, no mortal could tell. The gun was a sixteen repeater, and the man using it could have gotten in sixteen good shots before re-loading-- in case he had the time before the other fella got him.

Another true event was in the shape of a conversation. It was about three or four o'clock postmeridian when Cap. McCoach said to the writer --

"The *Western World* will have lots to write about this week -- wonder what it will have to say."

Before we could answer the dare-devil Maxwell broken in with ⸚

"Well, he better look out what he writes."

"We shall tell just what happened," we replied when Thompson remarked⸚

"Konkel is all right ⸚ we've nothing to fear from him."

Another event we overlooked in the Jack Fisher story was that Bill Rowan, who for the time was guarding Jack, was wanting to get out and help Maxwell and Thompson round things up and said to Ed Jennings ⸚

"Ed, I m going to leave you in charge of Jack for a while ⸚ and we'll hold you responsible for him."

"He ll be here when you come back," said Ed, and Bill went on out.

"Jack, I'm sorry for you," said Ed, after Bill was gone; but you know I ve got to keep you here till one of them comes back."

"It's all right Ed," said Jack "and thank you"

More Next time[194]

The Final Boston Grand Round-Up

Actual Happenings

Under the caption "Last Night" the *Western World* gave the following account of the epochal event of the day:

The first of the week Bill Thompson, Ed Maxwell and Bill Rowan and, with five other men, came up from the strip. They were armed with Winchesters, and said they owned a horse claimed by Tom O'Neal and Vandyke. They took five more horses that they claimed. This was done on Wednesday. Wednesday night a number of our citizens fired on Maxwell as he was leaning against a post of the awning in front of the saloon. Eight buckshot hit the post, which saved his life. His necktie was torn off. Five of the cow boys had gone to the strip with horses.

Thompson and Rowan were in the saloon; also Cox and his son -- the saloon keeper, and Ed Jennings, John McCoach, and a Mr. Bush.

About a dozen shots were fired into the saloon, and Bush, Jennings, and McCoach had a narrow escape.

As soon as Maxwell got back into the saloon he and Thompson and Rowan ran out at the side door and begin to shoot. Over a hundred shots were probably fired.

Wright's store was badly demolished and set on fire, but on the further consideration they put the fire out.

The fighting commenced about half-past 10 o clock and the shooting continued until nearly 2 o clock.

Today Thompson, Maxwell, and Rowan have gathered up all the arms they could find, and are hunting for some particular parties who were in on the shooting. The issue of this paper is delayed one day, and on Friday all is quiet and nothing more has been done. – **Western World**

What became of Everybody -- next week.[195]

Chapter 19: What Became of "Everbody"?

"The depopulation of Boston is now complete, Bill Thompson and his gang of toughs seem to have done this job fully well. It seems a strange occurrence, however that a few bullies can go into a civilized community and absolutely drive off everybody in one short week."

-The Richfield Monitor, April 1889

In the immediate aftermath of the Grand Roundup few details are available about what happened to most of the citizens of Boston after the April 1889 siege. Sam Konkel left for several years and returned to his homestead in 1905. He then bought the Springfield paper in 1913. We will defer most of the commentary of what happened to everybody to Konkel, but first, we will offer insight to those who seemed to vanish.

There are clues indicating Boston residents immediately following the siege stopped at Westola and Richfield, Kansas if only for a brief time before leaving the country. Doc Brown, after his harrowing escape from the regulators, was in Westola, Kansas a few days after the siege.[196]

> Dr. A. J. Brown of Boston, was on our streets Friday.

Even the "Jenningses" were unnerved by the siege as the following report from Coldwater, Kansas attests,[197]

> **Frank Je nings, formerly of this
> city, but later of Boston, Colorado, is
> said to have passed through Avilla a
> few days since and slept two nights in
> a barn. He used a Winchester for his
> pillow, and appeared to be startled at
> the waving of the grass.**

The Oklahoma 1889 land rush had just begun and many it appears were heading for those opportunities. [198] [199]

> Mr. W. H. Yaw and wife arrived here
> from Boston, Colorado, Thursday morn-
> ing, from where they had been driven by
> a band of desperadoes, so Mr. Yaw says.
> These ruffins had been carrying every-
> thing there with a high hand, holding up
> the banker, driving off stock, etc. The
> Boston citizens should organize and pro-
> tect their rights and liberty.

If not heading for new opportunities, they were at least getting
out as shown in the following report from West Plains, Kansas. The
boom was over.

> —Parties from Boston, Colo., passed
> through town last Sunday. They say
> that the town of Boston is "busted," and
> the people all leaving.

Mr. Price, editor of the Richfield Republican, informed us Saturday that Boston, Colorado had been terrorized by a band of cowboys who drove out the Mayor, Editor and all the leading citizens. Most of them came to Richfield. We have not been able to get any later news that was authentic.

Mr. John Harrelson and family, former residents of this place, but who have resided near Boston, Colorado for over a year, arrived here Sunday, bound for Oklahoma. Mr. H. has a brother there who has been a boomer for four years.

The siege of Boston began April 9, and these folks were gone by the 12th. The exodus from Boston had begun.[200]

The most visible sign Old Boston was abandoned came almost 90 years after the siege. On Oct 26, 1978, an Action to Quiet Title to Land notice appeared in Baca County's Plainsman Herald. A quiet title action is a legal (court) proceeding to determine who owns which rights in a tract of land. The proceeding is started when there is a conflict or uncertainty regarding who owns the legal interest in a tract of property, such as more than one person claiming ownership of the property. In this case it was the abandonment of the property by the original owners.

Nearly 500 property owners just walked away from Old Boston, never to return. This property sold, but there was uncertainty as to the real owners. To ensure no future claims are made against the property this action was taken to ensure the present owners would have full rights to the land after purchasing this property.

A full listing of the original property owners named in this action is in Appendix 2. There you will see many names you recognize from this story.

George Daniel is one of the few who left some evidence of a life after Boston. Sam writes about him, and I have included a few references as he seemed to have found a few more exciting times as the Denver Postal inspector. In 1915 it was reported,

"George Daniel, who has just assumed charge of his new office as post office inspector in charge of the Denver district, is a Denver man, although he has been located in New York, St. Louis and Cheyenne."[201]

He is even mentioned as the postal inspector in a 1916 edition of the Swedish Colorado Newspaper.[202]

The final reference to Daniel might be one of the more exciting events a postal inspector of the early 1900's might find.

"George Daniel, post office inspector, was notified by Celia V. Hagman, postmistress at Alma, in Park County, that the Alma post office burned."[203]

Finally, his experience in Old Boston might have prepared him well for this one,[204]

The Loveland postoffice this morning received the following order:
PERSONAL ATTENTION—DANGER
Postmaster:
Recent reports indicate that firearms, cartridges and explosives are occasionally being transported by the mails. In one instance a parcel containing six sticks of dynamite was mailed at a small office, traversed a star route and several hundred miles of railway route before being discovered and safely withdrawn.
Such things are dangerous and in violation of law.
No parcel should be accepted until the contents are known in order to see that the postal laws are not being violated.
GEORGE DANIEL,
Postoffice Inspector-in-Charge.

One citizen, J. N. Smith, mentioned by Konkel in his closing write ups about Old Boston appears to be a detail Sam did not remember correctly. The June 28, 1888 issue of the, *Rolla (Missouri) Herald* indicates Smith was a licensed Methodist preacher, was a Sunday School Superintendent in Boston and that he left a widow and a small child.[205]

References to anyone other than the "Jenningses" and George Daniel are scarce. Konkel discusses the time after Boston and what happened to everyone as follows,

"What became of everybody" has reference to those con-nected directly or indirectly with the final Boston Grand Roundup.

We'll begin with Ed Maxwell the dare-devil of the Cow boys rounding up the town. The story is told that Maxwell afterward lost his nerve, and that almost any kind of kid could kick him out of the house or pound him over the head, just as he did Lou Reeder in the one case, and Jack Fisher in the other. We don't know how much of the fact there is in the story, but we presume a sudden shock of some kind might produce such a result.

The last that was heard of him by people in Baca County was he was in Wyoming, about fifteen years ago, in the mining district of the Black Hills where we presume he was passing life by holding a better hand than the other feller; and it's just possible that it was the shock of a six shooter in the hands of the other feller that got his nerve.

Bill Thompson who furnished the brains and the treachery for the outfit, kept right on being a cow boy, a deputy sheriff, a U.S. marshal, etc. and largely in the interest of the Prairie Cattle Co., up to the time of his death.

Bill finally died with his boots on-- don't know as we can quite say that as he lived two or three days after receiving his death wound.

The paradox of his life was that having lived mostly as a debauched man-killer, his career was suddenly halted, and finally wound up as a peacemaker.

A certain young fellow and another fellow, we believe at the headquarters of the Prairie Cattle Company on the Picketwire, were in deadly combat or something of the kind, when Bill wedged himself in between them and implored them in the name of the saints and the apostles to turn from the error of their ways and to cease whittling on each other when he accidentally caught a bullet from one of their guns -- intended for the other feller.

We haven t learned as to whether the two antagonistos then ceased from the turmoil and lent their good offices to the fallen peacemaker and hero; or if they whittled and shot themselves up first and then waited on the fallen friend -- for Thompson was a friend to each.

Thompson lingered for some days after the shooting, and then got into the ferry boat with Father Time and crossed over the dark river to join the cow boys whom father time had already ferried across the stream.

Bill Rowan makes out the other member of the trinity of cow boys rounding up the town. Bill continued to live in No-Man's land on the Cimarron and when it was put on the market after Oklahoma became a state. He filed on the land he was living on and continued in the stock business.

We don t know just what property Rowan had gathered about him, but we presume he had a good many head of both horses and cattle. It is something now like 20 years ago that Rowan cashed in his chips, probably crossing over to have a talk with Bill Thompson on how best to round something up.

Bill had some trouble with one of his neighbors over the line between them or something of the sort, and one day he was found at or near the fence line with a bullet through him.

The neighbor was brought to trial, but there was no evidence connecting him with the shooting and was acquitted.

And we are wondering if Bill Rowan will be as lucky when he finally stands trial up yonder for that Boston roundup and other trivial things he did while journeying through this earthly veil of tears.

Ditto next week[206]

The Final Boston Grand Round-Up

What Became of Everybody

"He who fights and runs away, will live to fight another day."

The Israelitish army fought and ran away, but we haven't heard of any return engagement. -- though so far
as we know all of them may have been mixed up in the
Spanish-American war, and each of them may have been in
many a famous personal encounter since that time.

There are only five of the citizen soldiers we shall mention in this closing article of the old-time write-ups -- Doc
Brown, Geo Daniel, Lou Reeder, Jack Fisher and J. N.
Smith. As stated before none of the twenty of the citizen
army ever came back to old Boston or to Baca County, after
the wild gunplay that precipitated the grand Boston
roundup we've for some time been talking about.

Doc Brown moved to Missouri where he again went into
the drug business, and the last heard of him, in spite of
five or six burnouts, -- as it was related to us, he had made
good money, being worth at that time anywhere from
$10,000 to $50,000.

Gaul ran the *Boston Banner* for a while after George
left that night.[207] The plant was taken to Johnson City
Kans., and from there to Manzanola, Colo.

As stated before, Geo. Daniel was genial and popular,
and withal was possessed a foresight and pluck.

Without practically a dollar in his pocket and with a
family of five we believe on his hands and in a night's

time, he had something before him that will give you some idea of what about everybody in the country at that time was facing.

We understand that he drifted to Denver, and after a time got a job as a streetcar conductor.

Our next information was that he had joined the navy, and while in that capacity wrote a book -- presumably on seafaring life, but so far as we know both of those reports may have missed the facts about as far as Cook missed the North Pole.

At present, Daniel is post office inspector, with head-quarters at Denver, and of course is getting a good salary.

It doesn't take long to tell about Lou Reeder, as nothing is ever heard from him the night he "fought and ran away," to the present time.

As we have already told, he was raised by the Jenningses who, as everybody knows afterward became notorious outlaws, but in their outlaw life no mention has been made of Lou Reeder, and so far as we know they may have never gotten together again after that frightful night.

Jack Fisher -- Poor Jack Fisher! Was never heard of again, so far as our information goes, after that night. He came from Kentucky, and we presume he returned to Kentucky.[208]

J. N. Smith, the grocer on the corner whose store, Wright Grocery, was set a fire and the fire afterward put out by the cow boys. He likely returned to Missouri. He had a large family, and no doubt fought many and uphill and downhill battle before again getting onto his feet.[209]

What a sad commentary on life is the fact that the young folks of those old days, ranging from twenty to thirty, are now old men and women, running along in the neighborhood of fifty and sixty years, some of them prob-ably even grandpas and grandmas-- and only yesterday themselves of the young set.

Good People, readers of the Herald, this is the finis of the old-time write-ups.

We ve enjoyed it, have you?[210]

Chapter 20: After Boston

"The cowboys hated to give Boston up. It was a fine drinking and gambling town."

-Uncle Bill Thompson, 1935

J.R. Austin's work on recording the early history of Baca County has been the foundation for any subsequent writings on this topic.

He calls the time after the demise of Boston the dormant years for Baca County. Except for Springfield and Vilas, none of the towns had more than a post office, and most of the boom towns of 1886 - 1889 ceased to exist.

By 1890 there were only 1,479 people left out of a reported 6,000 citizens which arrived the previous four years. The newly formed county was already feeling the effects of the fighting, fraud and jealousy and one of the most newsworthy events of the new counties existence was yet to come, the burning of the Boston Hotel. The hotel which had been purchased to become the new courthouse for Baca County became the final newsworthy chapter in story of Old Boston.

Austin was a teacher in Springfield, Colorado when he wrote *"An Early History of Baca County"* in 1936. It included a brief overview of Boston's history and is familiar to most locals. However, it lacks detail on many aspects of Old Boston's history which we include in this text.

Austin provides the following insight into the mystique and curiosity we feel for old towns which are no longer with us. In his excerpt below, only the towns of Springfield and Vilas exist today, the remnant of seventeen boomtowns which popped up on the Colorado prairie in 1886 and 1887. Austin wrote,

"Had the old towns of 1887 continued to exist, the interest in them would not be as great as it is today. There's something about a lost chapter in the natural procession of events that tradition loving Americans like to preserve as a treasure. The element of mystery makes it attractive. Early events in Springfield and Vilas do not excite the popular imagination; the towns that are here today, many of the old landmarks still exist,[211] the past has gradually merged into the present, and tradition has become a thing of common knowledge.

But with an old, forgotten town it is different. How entrancing it is to stand amid the ancient stone ruins and lose oneself in reverie to picture in the imagination the scenes that belong to long ago. Transcribed there on the lonely plains are the symbols of its past. The long spacious Main Street is still in evidence, the lone cross street begins boldly in the center of the town only to melt away into the plains as the ruins of the buildings no longer confined it to its course. Here the people rode into town, walked across the street greeted their neighbors and friends, and they commented on the current topics of interest. The long rows of stones on the corner may have been the proudest store in town. Another less imposing, may well have been the place where the transient patron sat for meals and dreamed of the places far away. There, goods were sold and precious money taken by the hard fisted proprietor in exchange. Still another place may have been a saloon where the stern faced bartender disposed of his wares and kept a steely eye on the more suspicious looking characters who frequented the place. How many quarrels may have started and ended here. Lastly, and most important of all, are the little dugouts partly filled with stones where there once were homes."

He experiences a feeling something is left undone; and that something should be done to make the memories of the place live again. Reverently, he goes away with a newborn desire to delve into the mysteries of the past; to accept the challenge which is brought to him from the secrets of the long, long ago."[212]

The story of the Boston hotel burning occurred after settling the county seat fight and after most citizens of Boston had left the county. However, because of the drama surrounding the hotel's move, it was always seen as a part of the county seat fight. In reality, it was just adding insult to injury of a stinging county seat loss for Boston. Sealing Boston's destiny after the April 1889 siege was the subsequent fall 1889 election confirming Springfield as the county seat. A group from Springfield, led by the new County Clerk, James Church was completing steps making Springfield the County Seat. They needed a building for a courthouse and in their rival town sat the most elegant building in the new county. Church, joined with a few Springfield citizens to buy the building. The moving of such a large building from a small town must have been obvious, but for unknown reasons, the structure loaded with no trouble on a trailer pulled by 20 or more teams of horses. As they began the slow trek toward Springfield, another Boston group decided it was time for one more challenge to Springfield's journey to establish a county government. The Boston Hotel move made it less than ten miles when a group of vigilantes which appeared to be from Boston overtook the armed party moving the building and gained control of the building. Fresh on the heels of a county seat fight over 100 papers from coast to coast reported the incident as part of the county seat fight with themes of stealing and violence. The *Evening Star* in Washington DC stated,

"Serious trouble exists between the towns of Boston and Springfield, Colorado, over the selection of the county seat of Baca County. Last Saturday night a party left Springfield for Boston, intending to steal the hotel building at that place which the Bostonians were intending to use as a county courthouse in case the legislature made Boston the county seat. Rollers were put under the building, which is the finest in the county and three stories high, and twenty teams were hitched to it. Inside the

building were stationed twelve men with Winchester rifles. The building was moved about five miles from Boston when the people of the latter place discovered the trick and immediately organized. They overtook the Springfield party and drove the garrison from the building, which they burned. Great excitement prevails, and more fighting is likely. "

Other newspapers as far away as Philadelphia and Los Angeles reported on the hotel burning in the county seat fight between the tiny Colorado towns of Springfield and Boston as follows.

A COLORADO FORT ON ROLLERS.

A COUNTY SEAT WAR CAUSES SERIOUS TROUBLE.

Twelve Men With Winchester Rifles, Stationed Inside of a Moving Building, Fire on the Enemy.

Word has been received of serious trouble between the towns of Boston and Springfield in Baca. Baca County was made from Las Animas county there has been strife between these two towns as to which should have the county seat. The act organizing the county provided that Springfield should be the county seat, and at the election held last fall, it is alleged that, by the *manipulation of the ballots, it was made the permanent county seat. The people of the town of Boston claim that Springfield has not the $5,000 worth of county property necessary to prevent the county seat from being moved by a minority vote this fall. The only available building for a county court house was a hotel building in Boston. A few weeks ago this was sold at sheriff's sale, and was bought in by Springfield parties. Saturday night a party left Springfield for Boston with machinery costing $1,000, intending to move the building to the former town and use as a court house, thus preventing the county seat issue being raised this fall by reason of prominent improvements being made. Rollers were put under the building, which is the finest in the county and three stories high, and twenty teams were hitched to it. Inside the house were twelve men with Winchester rifles. The building was moved about five miles toward Springfield, which is about twenty-five miles from Boston, when the people of the latter place discovered the trick and immediately organized. All available horses and rifles were brought into requisition and pursuit was made. Upon overtaking the party they commanded a halt, which was answered by "a volley of shots from the men in the building. The Boston crowd then fired, and after a fierce battle, which ended in the Springfield party being driven from the building. Coal oil was then procured and the floors of the building saturated, which was set on fire and entirely consumed. Great excitement prevails, But owing to the isolation of the towns,*

Springfield being fifty miles from Lamar, which is the nearest railroad station, news is hard to obtain. Several parties arrived here from Springfield last night and departed hurriedly after buying all the cartridges they could find in town. It is reported, that several parties were seriously injured in the fight and two killed, but the news is not authentic[213]

A COUNTY-SEAT WAR.

Two Colorado Towns Engaged in Bitter Strife.

LAMAR, Col., Sept. 25.—Word is received of a serious county-seat strife between the towns of Boston and Springfield in Baca county. Springfield secured the seat at the election held last fall. The only available building in the county for a court house, was a hotel building in Boston. A few weeks ago this was sold at a sheriff's sale, and bought by Springfield parties. Saturday night a party left Springfield for Boston to move the building to the former town, and use it as a court house, thus preventing the county-seat issue from being raised this fall. The building was moved about five miles toward Springfield, which is about twenty-five miles from Boston, when the people of the latter place discovered the trick and immediately organized. All the available horses and rifles were brought into requisition and pursuit made. Upon overtaking the party, a battle began, which ended in the Springfield party being driven from the building, which was then burned by the Bostonians. Great excitement prevailed, but owing to the isolation of the towns, news is hard to obtain. Several parties arrived here from Springfield last night and departed hurriedly after buying all the cartridges they could find in town. There is a report that several parties were seriously wounded and two killed during the fight, but no news was authentic.

Los Angeles Herald report on Boston Hotel.[214]

Again, Sam Konkel provides insight as he wrote of the grandeur of the hotel and then of its subsequent demise as follows:

The Boston Hotel

The hotel company was incorporated last week, the stock is all subscribed, and the big hotel will now be pushed to completion. -- *Boston Western World*, April 1887

Information has reached us that the hotel was sold Monday at Trinidad for $525 to Jas Ward. Now the question is to whom does the hotel belong? -- *Boston Western World*, March 1889.

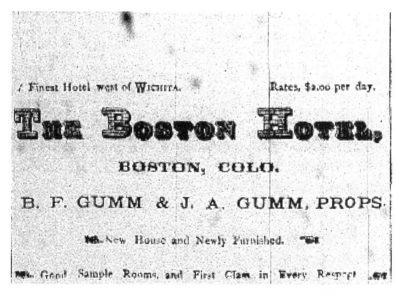

Gumm brothers March 1888 ad for The Boston Hotel[215]

The building of the Boston hotel was an epoch in old time events, the building becoming after built, the great civic and diplomatic center of the famous old town.

The building was about 40 x 60, three story, had something like 20 sleeping apartments and cost in the neighborhood of $10,000.

The facts are the hotel never paid a dollar on the investments. It was built during the summer of 1887, and by the time it was finished the far-seeing ones could easily begin to surmise that there were breakers on ahead for the thousands and thousands of good people in the highland west.

The leasee of the hotel, a Mr. Gumm, did fairly well during the winter of 87-88. Then immigration ceased, the money the boys brought with them was gone, there was nothing doing to enable anybody to earn more money, and the Gumm family being a very large one they were obliged to give up the hotel and to leave the country to make a living.

During the summer of 87 and winter of 87-88 there were several eating places in Boston, but one dropped out after another until the hotel was left and it was doing no business.

During all this time though the hotel remained a great civic and social center. Dances and various other social functions were scheduled at the hotel, often weekly, but probably averaging once a month.

Incidentally, at these dances the so-called cow boys of the neutral strip, particularly Billy the Kid, Bill Thompson and Ben Darnell were made much of, and certainly they should have felt grateful for their treatment, whether they did or not.

After the Gumm family left, the hotel fell into the hands of about three different leasees, not one of whom we suppose paid more than promises for the use of it, as there was just practically no money taken in to pay with.

During the summer of '88 people were pulling out by the hundred. '87 was the first year, and it was to be a sad crop and the season somewhat dry, the crop made nothing, and in '88 the people began to "gin it up" and to pull their freight.

Then came the final straw that broke the Boston camel's back -- the losing of the county seat. Everybody by this time knew that the country was a goner, and the days of the eternal city were numbered.

And there sat that great massive hotel, as a commentary on Burns' reverie on the plans of mice and men often going awry.

Who it belonged to we are not able at this time to say. Hughes had a controlling interest in it to start with, and he may afterwards have bought some of the interests of others, but it is not likely he did all of them. Hence the quandary as to whom the hotel actually belonged.

Whether it was sold to a fellow by the name of Ward or not isn't very material. Somebody finally sold it to Jim Church, E.K Curran and others of Springfield for $850, the intentions of the parties buying it being, as supposed, to saddle it onto the county at a fabulous price.

Having bought it, the next thing was to move it ⸗ and of course that was a long and tedious job. A regular moving outfit was secured, and slowly by horse power leverage and rope and pulleys the building was worming its way to its new location, and on a certain night after several days found itself on the south banks of the famous Sand Arroyo in the present old Christie pasture.

Also about one or two score of the men who weren't in sympathy with the saddling of a debt of $5,000 or such a matter on to the county for a building that cost a song, found the building at said night's resting place, overpowered the sleepy sentinels, told them to take their traps and hike it, and then in the course of an hour that hotel was furnishing the greatest bonfire the county has ever known.

And thus Jim Church, banker Curran and others didn't make a thousand per cent out of their investment off the county; and thus the famous Boston Hotel ended its famous career ⸗ just one of the links in the chain of the thousands and thousands of tragedies that were making history all over this rainless west in those days.[216]

Concluding the Old Boston, Colorado, story is Sam Konkel's vision for what Boston never had the chance to become. His optimism and dreams for the future of this town show in the March 8, 1888, edition of the *Western World*. He wrote the following article in anticipation of a November 27, 1897, ten-year anniversary celebration:

Joy Unconstrained.

A Day of Mingled Hilarity and Glorious and Rapturous Sport.

Boston Celebrates Its Tenth Anniversary in a Manner Becoming the Largest and Best City in Southeastern Colorado.

Boston Celebrates Its Tenth Anniversary in a Manner
Becoming the Largest and
Best City in Southeast Colorado.

The Presidential Party and Functionaries of State Lend
Their Presence and Review the Grand Procession. Presi-
dent Carlisle Christens, the City the Queen City of the
Plains, and the Philadelphia of the West

The Monstrous Procession is the Grandest ever Known
in the Grand Centennial State is Three Miles Long and is
Two Hours in Passing a Given Point

A Dozen Cities Roundabout Visit the Grand Metropolis
in Solid Phalanx, and go Away with Thankfulness in
Their Hearts and Eternal Praises on Their Lips

From Saturday's *Daily Western World,*
Nov. 24, 1897

Yesterday was a wild and rapturous day for Boston –
wild in mirth –rapturous in celebration and festivity. The
spirit of independence and liberty took possession of the
rollicking, tumultuous throng. The cool, bracing breeze
seemed to have caught up the inspiration and added to the
jollifications of the great anniversary by the clastic touch of
its magic and salubrious equanimity.

As the finger of the great town clock pointed the midnight hour, and beginning of the second decade of the city's
history, the report of a single gun from the dome of the
great court house broke the stillness; and then the tongues

of a hundred bells clanged out their stentorian notes, and were echoed and re-echoed by the somber stillness, the barking of dogs and the braying devotional exercises of a few long cared saints of the asinine creation that awoke to a meditation of coming events. Then the bells were stilled a moment, when the "Great Father" stepped to the receptacle in the parlor of the Grand Palace Hotel, lightly touched an electric knob, and instantly the lurid flames from the great gas wells lighted up the giant city with a glaring and dazzling light, followed by the belching roar of cannon and the stunning and deafening thud of the great nitro-dynamite guns.

The streets were soon alive with people, and when morning dawned the city was streaming with bunting banners, flags ensigns and a thousand and one other ornamentations, waving out a welcome of greeting to the whole world. Huge banners with "Welcome" in great gold letters crossed and recrossed every street and avenue. A great banner with a most beautiful pictorial illustration of "Boston ten years ago" formed a canopy over Main Street and Ninth Avenue.

By nine o'clock the streets were thronged with people. The first excursion train came in over the Rock Island. At eight o'clock three excursion trains came in over the B. T. W. from the west, and shortly after two more. The Santa Fe ran in other excursions from the east, and the N. K. N. M. from the northeast. A delegation from Springfield and vicinity came in overland, and likewise one from

Minneapolis, early in the day. Albany, Brookfield and Atlanta came in over the D. N. N. O. Every town in Southeastern Colorado, southwestern Kansas and the new state of Chiwawa was fairly represented.

At ten o'clock the procession was formed and the great parade commenced, headed by the Boston silver cornet band. One hundred of Boston's fair ones with white robes and on white steeds, two by two, formed the next link in the chain of the little misses dressed in white and bedecked with flowers. They followed by every trade, profession and business, headed by the great wholesale establishments of the city. The presidential party viewed the procession from the veranda of the Grand Central hotel at which point it started, and which it required two hours in passing. It entered Main street from west Ninth Avenue, passed south to and through the streets and avenues, northeast passed the machine shops and round house to the great Carlton oil and gas wells, and then north to the great Myron sugar refineries, the most extensive of any in the western states. Here a halt was made and a salute fired in honor of the founder of the establishment. The procession then moved northwest to the great artesian reservoir at the head of Lake Street, and by the Agricultural College west to the new court house, the most imposing structure in the southwest. From here it meandered to the point of starting and then north on Main Street it dragged its slow length to the union iron and smelting factories just building; then west to Trinity church at the head of Maple street, then southwest to 9th Avenue where it passed through the Grand Union park and around wholesale block east and north to the point of starting, where it disbanded after the third salute was fired in honor of the presidential party. The parade pro-nounced by visitors and spectators the grandest they ever witnessed.

The amusement of the afternoon were orations by the president, Senators Randal, Vilas and Teller, and General Sheridan, and speaker of the House Dickinson. Then came the ascension of the great automatic balloons with their cargos of human freight, which was kept up during the rest of the day.

At regular intervals during the whole day the roar and rattle of the cannons and the great nitro-dynamite guns and anvils rent the very air, and was carried away on its pliant wave to our neighboring allied towns, all others have long since found their goal in the sleep of sweet oblivion – turned up their toes to the daisies.

The great celebration closed at night with the grandest display of fireworks that has ever been witnessed in the west. For one hour the air was filled with skyrockets of every conceivable nature and description. A signal was fired and for one moment the great city was still, when the "Great Father" again placed his delicately carved index fin-ger on an electric knob – and air was filled with pinions, fire wheels, circles and such a variety of other fire displays as has been witnessed but once before in the history of the world. It was the second testing of the great Edison nitro-electric battery and automatic dynamo fire display. This was witnessed one hour, not only by the hundred thousand people in Boston on this celebrions and famous night, but by a hundred towns round about which distance only added grandeur and enchantment.

And thus closed the tenth anniversary and first decade of the history of the great "hub' of the southwest. It will never be forgotten, and by its great magnitude will send the fame of the city around the world.[217]

Epilogue

A Ten Year Anniversary wasn't to be for ol' Boston. After the April 1889 siege of the town, most people left. Sam Konkel moved the *Western World* to Lyons, Kansas. George Daniel sold the *Boston Banner* to L.D. Gaul who hung on for a couple more years. A few merchants such as the Burnett's also stayed on for a couple years. The postmaster, likely stayed for a few more years until the post office was officially closed. Boston was never intended to be a trail town or cow town. The town founders, Albert Hughes, Judge Jennings and the Jennings boys foresaw a grand and glorious hub for commerce and agriculture in southeast Colorado. But things didn't go as planned when the cow boys came to town. "The Utopian City of the Plains" quickly dissolved from the "Hub of the Universe" into the dystopian city of the plains, which among old west frontier towns was "As Wild As They Come," and thus was the end of Old Boston.

Appendix 1

Old Boston Colorado Timeline

Fall 1886 - Sam Konkel makes first trip to southeast Colorado and shortly thereafter established "Eagle Ranch," Colorado.

November 15, 1886 - Albert Hughes Judge Jenning, Al & Ed Jennings spend the night with Simeon Konkel Family.

November 16, 1886 - The Boston town site was surveyed and staked out, establishing the town of Boston.

March 1887- Sam Konkel starts the *Western World* Newspaper.

Summer 1887 - Geo. Daniel starts the *Boston Banner* Newspaper.

September 23, 1887 - A saloon keeper is shot and killed by an unknown man.

December 1887- Newt Bradley was killed after drunken encounter in Doc Brown's store.

December 31, 1887 - Amateur dramatic play "Ten Nights in a Bar Room."

February 1888 - It is reported Bill Thompson was killed by a horse thief, Jack White. This is a strange thread in the Boston story. We have documentation which shows Big Bill Thompson was at the final roundup of Boston in April 1889, in the cowboy funeral picture in 1891, and was killed in 1892 in Higbee, Colorado at the Headquarters of the Prairie Cattle Company.

September 6, 1888 - John Jennings leads detachment from Boston into the Neutral Strip after William Cornelius aka Billy the Kid. They overtake Cock-eyed Jones.

October 6 1888 - Henry Booth is shot and killed.

November 1888 - Booth widow is sent home after attempting to recover her dead husband's effects.

April 9, 1889 - Big Bill Thompson, Bill Rowan and Ed Maxwell and 5 heavily armed cow boys ride back into Boston for the final time. This is interesting to me. In all previous writings on Boston it seems it was only a short time between the Bradley killing and when these guys came back. It actually appears it could have been well over a year before they came back to avenge Bradley's death.

April 10, 1889 - Thompson Rowan and Maxwell are bushwhacked by a citizen's vigilante while in the saloon at the center of Boston.

July 1889 - Sam Konkel moves the *Western World* to Lyons, Kansas, renaming it the *Lyons Democrat*.

September 1890 – Boston Hotel is burned to the ground en route to Springfield.

October 26, 1978 - Action to Quiet Title to Land notice posted in the *Plainsman Herald*. An action to quiet title is a lawsuit brought in a court having jurisdiction over property disputes, in order to establish a party's title to real property, or personal property having a title, of against anyone and everyone, and thus "quiet" any challenges or claims to the title. As most residents of Boston just walked away from their property at some point after the siege of 1889, ownership of the property in the Boston Township was never really settled until this time.

Appendix 2

LEGAL NOTICES

IN THE DISTRICT COURT IN AND
FOR THE COUNTY OF BACA
AND STATE OF COLORADO
No. 78-CV-51

Action To Quiet
Title to Land
COMPLAINT UNDER
RULE 105

CHARLES M. RATCLIFF ESTATE,)
DELCIE N. and DALE E. RATCLIFF,)
CO-PERSONAL REPRESENTATIVES,)

Plaintiff,)

vs.

WALTER G. HINES, County Judge,
as Trustee for the Occupants of the
Townsite of Boston, Colorado

F. F. JENNINGS, W. O. P. McWORTER,
J. W. GIBSON, CHARLES EDLER, B. F.
GUMM, A. G. WILSON, S. H. PORKS,
WM. L. C. HAWK, J. J. BURNETT,
BULLINE MOORE & EMERY, ATLANTIS
TOWN CO., CALVIN FERGUSON,
WESTLEY FERGUSON, A. J. BROWN,
JOHN J. BENNETT, WALTER O. HINES,
WALTER G. HINES, SAM W. McCLURE,
OSCAR G. LEE, J. D. F. JENNINGS,
F. H. BOARDMAN, JOHN P. KEEN,
AUGUSTA CZAPANSKY, FERDINAND
CZAPANSKY, LOUIS WECKWORTH, R.
H. THOMAS, MARY E. THOMAS, ISA L.
JONES, BURNEY B. SIPE, JESSIE W.
EMERY, P. THEODORE WENKENS, J.
W. ROBINSON, JAMES T. THORNTON,
GREGORY GROCERY CO., A. J.
JENNINGS, D. H. SALINGER, J. N. SMITH,
R. F. DOLAN & CO., JAMES T.
THORNTON, HARLOW S. SWALLEY,
GEORGE B. WIDDERFIELD, WILLIAM
SHOMP, L. S. OWENS, W. T. BURNS,
JOHN D. MILLER, DELILA D.
HARTZELL, HENRY A. THOMPSON,
EMMA DURLAND, LAWRENCE S. OWEN,
CHARLES R. ELDER, EASTERN
COLORADO TOWN CO., LAURA J.
HAMBRICK, JOSEPH J. HONES, E. M.
WHITAKER, WILLIBOLD SIMMA, E. R.
BARBOUR, DORA E. POLAND,
MARCELLUS J. NEWMAN, LEWIS F.
MATHEWS, WILLIAM B. WRIGHT,
MARGARET E. DIGNAN, JOHN W.
GIBBS, D. E. DEPUTY, E. M. ELLIS,
LEWIS F. MATHEWS, SAMUEL M.
BENIGHT, MOLLIE C. EADS, ALBERT
HUGHES, AARON BEHRENDS, WILLIAM
H. YAW, MAGGIE E. DIGNAN, JOSEPH
G. CLAYTON, HATTIE V. MILLER, W.
CHOCKLEY, J. C. WARD, R. C. WINECUP,
A. F. HOLLENBECK, LEAH EVANS,

WALLIS & WIFE, ROBERT E. WAL-
LIS, JR, FERDINAND WESTHEIMER &
SONS, V. P. CONCANNON, B. T. GIT-
CHEL, LEWIS C. BACON, S. WILSON,
M. R. McCRORY, GARDNER MOTT, IDA
MOTT, GEORGE LAWYER, KATE C.
LAWYER, HENRY MOTT, J. W. GIBSON,
JAMES E. COX, JOHN G. LUHMAN,
FRANK W. BROOKE, I. M. WILCOX,
GARDNER MOTT, C. BRADFORD &
WIFE, THOMAS E. CAMERON, AL-
FRED A. MULLEN, JAMES A. EVANS,
JACOB C. GRADFORD, B. H. HOUSER,
WILLIAM MILLER, ROBERT CHAMPET,
THOS. E. YOUNG, ELTIE E. HOUSER,
BENJAMIN GRUMM, ALONZO BRYNING,
EDWARD A. KLOTE, AMSDEN LUMBER
COMPANY, GEORGE B. ELLIS, IRIS
G. ELLIS, JOSEPH H. PAYNE, SAM-
UEL M. KONKEL, SARAH M. UP-
DIKE, NATHAN A. WHITE, J. E. FISH-
BLAKE, BENJ. HOWERTH, C. L. BROWN,
COLUMBUS C. HENRY, NELSON MOLY-
NECOX, JOHN TAYLOR, ALICE BALD-
WIN, A. M. MILLARD, A. HUMMER,
ALFRED T. SPOTSWOOD, EDWARD L.
CAMPBELL, LAIR G. GALL, LEONIDAS
LAND, RICHARD N. WILCOX, H. E.
GORDON, G. J. HOFFMAN, ABRAHAM
DORBAUCH, ROBERT E. WALLIS &
WIFE, ROBERT E. WALLIS, JR., FERD-
INAND WESTHEIMER & SONS, V. P.
CONCANNON, B. T. GITCHEL, LEWIS C.
BACON, S. S. WILSON, M. R. McCRORY,
GARDNER MOTT, IDA MOTT, GEORGE
LAWYER, KATE C. LAWYER, HENRY
MOTT, J. W. GIBSON, JAMES E. COX,
JOHN G. LUHMAN, FRANK W. BROOKE
I. M. WILCOX, GARDNER MOTT C.
BRADFORD & WIFE, THOMAS E. CAM-
ERON, ALFRED A. MULLEN, JAMES A.
EVANS, JACOB C. GRADFORD, B. H.
HOUSER, WILLIAM MILLER, ROBERT
CHAMPET, THOS. E. YOUNG, ELTIE E.
HOUSER, BENJAMIN GRUMM, ALONZO
BRYNING, EDWARD A. KLOTE, AMSDEN
LUMBER COMPANY, GEORGE B. ELLIS,
IRIS G. ELLIS, JOSEPH H. PAYNE,
SAMUEL M. KONKEL, SARAH M.
UPDIKE, NATHAN A. WHITE, J. E. FISH-
ER, A. DARROCH, GEORGE W. WRIGHT,
THOMAS WHITE, WILL B. HUNTER,
JAMES D. CULVER, O. W. OTTEN,
FRANK H. LEPEL, MAY E. BENIGHT,
WILLIAM R. SMITH, JAMES D. CULVER,
COLUMBUS L. HENRY, B. F. SALYER,
EDWARD E. BLAKE, JOSEPH E.
HUNTER, ELIZABETH WARE, EMMA
CHAFFEE, GEORGE DANIEL, HENRY G.
SALYER, JAMES D. FAIR, DANIEL M.
STONECKER, ALEXANDER TAGGERT,
DAVID STONECKER, JOHN M. REMING-
TON, B. CHON, ELLA BLISARD,
THOMAS MURPHY, J. G. LUHEMAN,
S. E. SPEOULE, EBENEZER Mc-
DOWELL, D. CHAMNESS, T. F. BURSON,
CLARA F. RATCLIFF, FRANK F. ALL-
BEITTEN, TRUSTEE, HARRY BOVIE,
MARGARET BOVIE, BENJAMIN F. SIB-
LEY, JOHN E. WINER, WILLIAM H.

A, F. HOLLENBECK, LEAH EVANS, W. B. CHOCKLEY, ALBERT HUGHES, CHARLES M. ELLIS, JAMES C. WARD, E. C. ELRIDGE, BOSTON HOTEL CO., CHARLOTTE A. HUGHES, CHARLES A. CORYELL, HENRY S. DAVIS, C. E. ELDRIDE, CHARLES A. CORNELL, MARGARET A. FISH, JOSEPH N. JOBES, G. W. CAVANAUGH, LETELIA A. CAVANAUGH, F. W. CAVANAUGH, THOMAS MORAN, WILLIAM J. MINICH, JOHN D. MOTT, JOHN E. OTTEN, R. C. SMITH, ALLICE J. MOTT, RICHARD N. WILCOX, JOHN T. RAMEY, LOUIS REEDEN, N. N. McLEAN, FRANK S. KLOTE, LOUIS H. REEDER, I. N. WILCOX, WM. T. PAYNE, LIZZIE F. HOFFMAN, WILLIAM J. DARROCH, JOHN R. SCOTHORN, ALBERT HAWKINS, HERRIETTA HILL, JAMES L. BLEVINS, S. W. BRADWELL, JOHN C. KORNEZ, WILLIAM H. HARVIS, EMEL LEPEL, EMMA D. HAWK, JAMES T. MITCHELL. JOHN C. KIPPER, JOHN C. KOMER, WILLIAM M. SPENCER, F. C. MURRAY, W. H. LINDLEY, J. V. REED, THOMAS E. BERRY, WILLIAM T. TINSLEY, JOHN C. FISHER, H. M. TINKER, M. R. McCRORY, WILLIAM T. TUNLEY, ROBERT C. CARPENTER, JOHN C. KOMCA, A. A. ATHERTON, C. KIPPER, JACOB G. WARD, J. E. CRAW, ROBERT A. HAMBRICK, Q. A. ROBERTSON, AUGUST VOELZEL, HARLAN P. ORNDOFF, FRANK F.

HARLAN P. ORNDOFF, FRANK F. JAMES, JAMES F. MAHAFFEY, W. T. BURNS, JOHN C. MURPHY, ANDREW B. ALEXANDER, C. HICKMAN, JR. R. W. DEVINNY, ALEXANDER G. WILSON, OLIVE KELLOGG, F. THEODORE WINKINS, FRANK EXLINE, B. F. SPENCER, C. T. QUISENBERY, ALLEN M. HAMBRICK, W. T. SNYDER, E. H. BOARDMAN, ADAM N. SCHUSTER, JAMES W. KINGSTON, ROBERT A. HAMBRIC, ALLEN M. HAMBRIC, THOMAS W. HAMBRIC, FRANCIS HALL, ISSAC K. BERRY, THOMAS E. BERRY, WILLIAM T. SNYDER, L. A. PEYOR, SARAH HAMBRIC, CHARLES C. LOGSDON, MRS. LOGSDON, J. H. CONCANNON, L. U. HUMPHRY, CASSIUS C. COX, KENNETH W. ALLISON, W. M. BEATY, ETTIE R. HILL, NELSON MOLGNEUZ, JOHN TAYLOR, WILLIROLD SIMMA, GEORGE T. GUERNSEY, JEROME W. KLEYLA, WILLIAM O. LEHMAN, GEORGE L. MURPHY, WILLIAM MILLER, MAMMIE MORRISSMITH, WILLIAM F. DOLAN, JULIA R. HORAN, JULIA R. HORAN, LOUISIANA T. SWELLEY, CORNELIUS HICKMAN, A. M. COFFMAN, JOHN D. MOTT, E. F. MOTT, J. N. WILCOX, JOHN H. RAMSEY, ARTHUR GIBSON, JAMES R. SNOW, HENRY J. JeCOMB, B. W. PICKETT, EDGAR E. JENNINGS, WILLIAM I. McKAIG, JOHNSON AND LAMMER E. G. COMPANY, EMIL WEDERMUHER, O. L. STOCKWELL, C. O. BLAKE BEN, HOWERTH, C. L. BROWN, COLUMBUS C. HENRY, NELSON MOLYNECOX, JOHN TAYLOR, ALICE BALDWIN, A. M. MILLARD, A. HUMMER, ALFRED T. SPOTSWOOD, EDWARD L. CAMPBELL, LAIRG. GALT, LEONIDAS LAND, RICHARD N. WILCOX, H. E. GORDON, C. J. HOFFMAN, ABRAHAM DORRAUCH, ROBERT E.

MARGARET BOVIE, BENJAMIN F. SIBLEY, JOHN E. WINER, WILLIAM R. CONRAD, HELLENN POLLEY, HENRY W. STIFF, J. D. NEWTON, F. J. NEWTON, NORMA A. McLEAN, GREEN H. STROTLEE, GEORGE M. METTERCUTT, L. F. MATHEWS, H. H. McMASTERS, FRANK M. DOBER, JOHN M. PENNINGTON, R. C. SMITH, PARKER SHEPARD, C. M. JEROME, N. N. McLEAN, NELL R. HUNTER, MARY L. HUNTER, C. M. ELLIS, JACOB L. CHISM, HIRAM S. LAPHAM, CITIZENS' BANK, TRINIDAD, COLO., BANK OF RICHFIELD, KANSAS, CLAUDE JONES, RALPH HOOKER, MARGARET MAXWELL, WILLIAM HOOKER, T. ELDEN ALLEN, KATE ALLEN, FRANK ROBERTS, HOMER F. THOMPSON, AND ALL UNKNOWN PERSONS WHO) CLAIM ANY INTEREST IN THE SUB-) JECT MATTER,) DEFENDANTS)

1. The Plaintiff is the owner and in possession of the following described real property situate in Baca County, Colorado:

The Southeast Quarter of the Southeast Quarter (SE1/4SE1/4) of Section Twenty-one (21); The Southwest Quarter of the Southwest Quarter (SW1/4SW1/4) of Section Twenty-two (22); the Northwest Quarter of the Northwest Quarter (NW1/4NW1/4) of Section Twenty-seven (27); the Northeast Quar-

ter of the Northeast Quarter (NE1/4NE1/4) of Section Twenty-eight (28); All in Township Thirty-two (32) South, Range Forty-four (44) West of the 6th P.M., also known and described as the Original Town of Boston, Colorado.

2. The deceased, Charles M. Ratcliff, has been in open, continuous, exclusive, adverse and notorious possession of the above described real property under color of title to said property since October 8, 1949 to the date of his death.

3. There may be persons interested in the subject matter of this action whose names cannot be inserted herein because said names are unknown to the plaintiff although diligent efforts have been made to ascertain the names of said persons; such persons have been made defendants and designated as "all unknown persons who claim any interest in the subject matter of this action," so far as plaintiff's knowledge extends; the interests of the unknown parties are derived through some one or more of the named defendants.

4. The defendants claim some right, title, or interest in and to the above described real property adverse to plaintiff; the claims of said defendants are without foundation or right.

WHEREFORE, plaintiff prays for a complete adjudication of the rights of all parties to this action with respect to the real property above described; for a decree requiring defendants to set forth the nature of their claims, determining that the defendants and each of them have no interest, estate, or claim of any kind whatsoever in the said real property, forever barring and enjoining the defendants from asserting any claim or title thereto, quieting the title of the plaintiff in and to the real property and adjudging

Appendix 3

Letter to the Editor on Konkel's old time write ups:

F. C. Stalnaker of Centerville, Kansas, in a letter on other matters, says they have kept a complete file of the Herald since the "old time" write ups started the first part of the year. As near as we can get a line-up, our readers regardless of whether they were ever in old Boston or not, or even in Baca County or Colorado, watch anxiously from week to week for the old time write ups and read it before reading anything else.

Springfield Herald **(Springfield, CO) Oct 4, 1918**

Glossary

Notes

[1] Photo courtesy of the Baca County Museum, Springfield, Colorado.
[2] Photo courtesy of the Denver Public Library, Denver, Colorado.
[3] Bryan, Carroll G. *GENEALOGY and HISTORY of the DESCENDANTS of WILLIAM KONKEL.* Detroit, MI: Boulevard Press, 1966.
[4] *Kiowa County Signal* (Greensburg, Kansas) Friday Mar 18, 1887, Page 1.
[5] *The Girard Press* (Girard, Kansas) · Thu, Mar 31, 1887 · Page 3.
[6] *Belle Plaine News* (Belle Plaine, Kansas) · Sat, Mar 24, 1888 · Page 3.
[7] Sam Konkel photos provided courtesy of Zaylan Konkel.
[8] Konkel, Sam. *Springfield Herald* (Springfield, Colorado) January 9, 1914.
[9] Konkel, Sam. "Persons, Stories and Incidents of Old Boston and the Old Days." *Springfield Herald* (Springfield, Colorado) Nov 8, 1918.
[10] Konkel, Sam. "Persons, Stories and Incidents of Old Boston and the Old Days." *Springfield Herald* (Springfield, Colorado) Nov 12, 1918.
[11] Konkel, Sam. "Persons, Stories and Incidents of Old Boston and the Old Days." *Springfield Herald* (Springfield, Colorado) Oct 21, 1918.
[12] Konkel, Sam. "Persons, Stories and Incidents of Old Boston and the Old Days." *Springfield Herald* (Springfield, Colorado) January 18, 1918.
[13] Konkel, Sam. "Persons, Stories and Incidents of Old Boston and the Old Days." *Springfield Herald,* (Springfield, Colorado) Jan 18, 1918.
[14] This refers to Springfield, Kansas rather than Springfield, Colorado.
[15] Konkel, Sam. "Persons, Stories and Incidents of Old Boston and the Old Days." *Springfield Herald* (Springfield, Colorado) Jan 25, 1918.
[16] *The Baltimore Sun* (Baltimore, Maryland) · Mon, Apr 15, 1889, · Page 4.
[17] The *Los Angeles Times* (Los Angeles, California) · Sun, Apr 14, 1889, Page 5.
[18] "Baca County." Baca County, Baca County Historical Society, 1983, p. 407.
[19] *Western World* (Boston, Colorado), March 8, 1888. Baca County Museum, Springfield, Colorado.
[20] *Western World* (Boston, Colorado), March 8, 1888. Baca County Museum, Springfield, Colorado.
[21] *Medicine Lodge* Cresset (Medicine Lodge, Kansas) · Thu, Mar 10, 1887
[22] *Greensburg Rustler* (Greensburg, Kansas) · 04 Aug 1887, Thu · Page 3
[23] *The Lexington Leader* (Lexington, Kansas) · 01 Apr 1887, Fri · Page 4
[24] Konkel, Sam. "Persons, Stories and Incidents of Old Boston and the Old Days." *Springfield Herald* (Springfield, Colorado) January 11, 1918.
[25] Konkel, Sam. "Persons, Stories and Incidents of Old Boston and the Old Days." *Springfield Herald* (Springfield, Colorado) January 7, 1918.
[26] *The Citizen* (Trinidad, Colorado) 10 Nov 1887.
[27] *Seward County Courant* (Springfield, Kansas) · 09 Sep 1887, Fri · Page 5.
[28] *Greensburg Rustler* (Greensburg, Kansas) · 04 Aug 1887, Thu · Page 3.
[29] *The Taloga Star* (Taloga, Kansas) · 11 Nov 1887, Fri · Page 3.
[30] *The Citizen* (Trinidad, Colorado) 10 Nov 1887.
[31] *Western World* (Boston, Colorado), March 8, 1888. Baca County Museum, Springfield Colorado.
[32] *Boston World* (Boston Colorado) · Thurs March 8, 1888 · Page 1.
[33] Konkel, Sam. "Persons, Stories and Incidents of Old Boston and the Old Days." *Springfield Herald* (Springfield, Colorado) January 10, 1918.
[34] The *Leader-Democrat* (Richfield, Kansas) · 30 Apr 1887, Sat · Page 3.

[35] The Citizen (Trinidad Colorado) · Nov 25, 1887
[36] *Coldwater Review* (Coldwater, Kansas) · 19 Aug 1887, Fri · Page 7.
[37] The *Leader-Democrat* (Richfield, Kansas) · 18 Dec 1886, Sat · Page 3.
[38] The Leader-Democrat (Richfield, Kansas) · 12 Jan 1889, Sat · Page 3.
[39] Jennings, Al. *Beating Back.* Curtis Publishing, 1913.
[40] Konkel, Sam. "Persons, Stories and Incidents of Old Boston and the Old Days." *Springfield Herald* (Springfield, Colorado) March 29, 1918.
[41] Jennings, Al J, and Will Irwin. "BEATING BACK - The Long Riders." Saturday Evening Post, 20 Sept. 1913, p. 21.
[42] *The Citizen* (Trinidad Colorado) 10 Nov 1887.
[43] Konkel, Sam. "Persons, Stories and Incidents of Old Boston and the Old Days." *Springfield Herald* (Springfield, Colorado) April 5, 1918
[44] Photo courtesy of Courtesy of the Oklahoma Historical Society, Al Jennings 4268.B 1906.
[45] Temple Houston was actually the youngest child of Magaret Lea and Sam Houston.
[46] Konkel, Sam. "Persons, Stories and Incidents of Old Boston and the Old Days." *Springfield Herald* (Springfield, Colorado) April 12, 1918.
[47] Konkel, Sam. "Persons, Stories and Incidents of Old Boston and the Old Days." *Springfield Herald,* November 12, 1918.
[48] Konkel, Sam. "Persons, Stories and Incidents of Old Boston and the Old Days." *Springfield Herald* (Springfield, Colorado) November 22, 1918.
[49] Austin, J. R. "The Old Towns." *A History of Early Baca County,*1936.
[50] *Boston Banner* (Boston, Colorado), May 26, 1888. Courtesy of the Baca County Museum, Springfield, Colorado.
[51] *Ashland Clipper* (Ashland, Kansas) · Thu, Dec 11, 1884 · Page 3.
[52] Jennings, Al J, and Will Irwin. "BEATING BACK - The Long Riders." Saturday Evening Post, 20 Sept. 1913, p. 21.
[53] Jennings & Jennings. "Attorneys at Law," Advertisement. *Boston Banner* (Boston, Colorado), May 26, 1888.
[54] J. Jennings. "Attorney at Law," *Western World* (Boston, Colorado) March 8, 1888.
[55] Jennings, Al J, and Will Irwin. "BEATING BACK - The Long Riders." *Saturday Evening Post*, 20 Sept. 1913, p. 21
[56] They abandoned their interests. See Quiet Claim Deed in Appendix 2.
[57] Everywhere else the hotel is listed as a $10,000 including in the March 1888 *Western World.*
[58] Konkel, Sam. "Persons, Stories and Incidents of Old Boston and the Old Days." *Springfield Herald* (Springfield, Colorado) March 15, 1918.
[59] J.A. Brown. "General Merchandise" Advertisement. *Boston Banner* (Boston Colorado), May 26, 1888.
[60] T. Hambric. "Dealer in Hardware Stoves and Tinware" Advertisement. *Boston Banner* (Boston, Colorado), May 26, 1888.
[61] Konkel, Sam. "Persons, Stories and Incidents of Old Boston and the Old Days." *Springfield Herald* (Springfield, Colorado) Mar 22, 1918.

[62] Konkel, Sam. "Persons, Stories and Incidents of Old Boston and the Old Days." *Springfield Herald* (Springfield, Colorado) Mar 22, 1918.
[63] *The Western Star* (Coldwater, Kansas) · 18 Oct 1884, Sat · Page 3

[64] Photo courtesy of Dr. Milligan's great grandson Michael Clark.
[65] Dr. W.L.C. Hawk. "Physician & Surgeon." Advertisement. *Boston Banner* (Boston, Colorado), March 8, 1888.
[66] Konkel, Sam. "Persons, Stories and Incidents of Old Boston and the Old Days." *Springfield Herald* (Springfield, Colorado) December 6, 1918.
[67] R.B Whitaker. "Attorney at Law and Notary Public" Advertisement. *Boston Banner* (Boston, Colorado), March 8, 1888.
[68] Konkel, Sam. "Persons, Stories and Incidents of Old Boston and the Old Days." *Springfield Herald* (Springfield, Colorado) December 13, 1918.
[69] Photo courtesy of the Baca County Museum, Springfield CO.
[70] Konkel, Sam. "Persons, Stories and Incidents of Old Boston and the Old Days." *Springfield Herald* (Springfield, Colorado) November 22, 1918.
[71] The *Leader-Democrat* (Richfield, Kansas) · 26 Feb 1887, Sat · Page 3.
[72] William H. Yaw. "Brand Notice, Advertisement. *Western World* (Boston, Colorado), March 8, 1888.
[73] Notice Yaw's address is listed the Neutral Strip although he did run a livery business in Boston
[74] Konkel, Sam. "Persons, Stories and Incidents of Old Boston and the Old Days." *Springfield Herald* (Springfield, Colorado) September 20, 1918.
[75] Konkel, Sam. "Persons, Stories and Incidents of Old Boston and the Old Days." *Springfield Herald* (Springfield, Colorado) Sept 27, 1918.
[76] Konkel, Sam. "Persons, Stories and Incidents of Old Boston and the Old Days." *Springfield Herald* (Springfield, Colorado) November 22, 1918.
[77] Konkel, Sam. "Persons, Stories and Incidents of Old Boston and the Old Days." *Springfield Herald* (Springfield, Colorado) October 4, 1918.
[78] The *Richfield Monitor* (Richfield, Kansas) · 07 Sep 1888, Fri · Page 3.
[79] The Garden City Herald (Garden City, Kansas) · 08 Jun 1922, Thu · Page 8.
[80] The *Leader-Democrat* (Richfield, Kansas) · 11 Aug 1888, Sat · Page 3.
[81] Konkel, Sam. "Persons, Stories and Incidents of Old Boston and the Old Days." *Springfield Herald* (Springfield, Colorado) October 11, 1918.
[82] *Ashland Clipper* (Ashland, Kansas) Thu, Feb 9, 1888 · Page 8.
[83] Konkel, Sam. "Persons, Stories and Incidents of Old Boston and the Old Days." *Springfield Herald* (Springfield, Colorado) October 5, 1918
[84] Konkel, Sam. "Persons, Stories and Incidents of Old Boston and the Old Days." *Springfield Herald* (Springfield, Colorado) Nov 1, 1918.
[85] Konkel, Sam. "Persons, Stories and Incidents of Old Boston and the Old Days." *Springfield Herald* (Springfield, Colorado) September 12, 1918.
[86] Konkel, Sam. "Persons, Stories and Incidents of Old Boston and the Old Days." *Springfield Herald* (Springfield, Colorado) September 20, 1918.
[87] *Garden City Sentinel* (Garden City, Kansas) · 29 Sep 1888, Sat · Page 5.
[88] Konkel, Sam. "Persons, Stories and Incidents of Old Boston and the Old Days." *Springfield Herald* (Springfield, Colorado) November 29, 1918.
[89] The *Leader-Democrat* (Richfield, Kansas) · 11 Aug 1888, Sat · Page 3.
[90] *Coldwater Review* (Coldwater, Kansas) · 16 Jun 1885, Tue · Page 7
[91] Turner, Kenneth R. "No Man's Land". Encyclopedia of Oklahoma History and Culture. Oklahoma Historical Society.
[92] *The Sun* (New York, NY) · Sun, Jan 20, 1889 · Page 7. Library of Congress.
[93] *Ashland Clipper* (Ashland, Kansas) · Thu, Oct 15, 1885 · Page 3.

[94] *The Sun* (New York, New York) · Sun, Jan 20, 1889 · Page 7. Library of Congress.

[95] The *Dallas Daily Herald* (Dallas Texas) 30 Aug. 1881.

[96] Thompson's Kid got the name because he at one time rode with the Regulator Bill Thompson. His real name was either Fred Horton or Fred Houghton.

[97] Bold Horse Thieves." The Topeka Daily Capital, 29 Aug. 1888, p. 1.

[98] *The Hutchinson News* (Hutchinson, Kansas) · Wed, Feb 27, 1889·Page 1

[99] The *Leavenworth Weekly Times* (Leavenworth, Kansas) · Thu, Sep 20, 1888 · Page 8.

[100] The *Springfield Republican*, (Springfield, Colorado) Tuesday June 1, 1937.

[101] The *Richfield Monitor* (Richfield, Kansas) · 07 Sep 1888, Fri · Page 3.

[102] The *Richfield Monitor* (Richfield, Kansas) · 07 Sep 1888, Fri · Page 2.

[103] The *Richfield Monitor* (Richfield, Kansas) · 07 Sep 1888, Fri · Page 2.

[104] The *Richfield Monitor* (Richfield, Kansas) · 07 Sep 1888, Fri · Page 2.

[105] The *Coffeyville Weekly Journal*, (Coffeyville Kansas) Thursday Dec 20, 1888.

[106] *Fort Morgan Times*, Volume V, Number 2, Sept, 6 1888. Page 1. Colorado Historic Newspapers Collection. Colorado State Library.

[107] *Leadville Evening Chronicle* Sept, 6 1888. Page 1. Colorado Historic Newspapers Collection. Colorado State Library.

[108] Konkel, Sam. "Persons, Stories and Incidents of Old Boston and the Old Days." *Springfield Herald* (Springfield, Colorado) May 10, 1918.

[109] Lepel Brothers. "Boston Blacksmith and Carriage Shop, Advertisement. *Boston Banner* (Boston, Colorado), March 8, 1888.

[110] This lines up with Alberta Clark's recollection as the ZH ranch was northwest of present Boise City, Oklahoma which was at the time the Neutral Strip or No Man's land.

[111] NOTE: There are some references of this being his uncle's house outside of Springfield, Colorado.

[112] Konkel, Sam. "Persons, Stories and Incidents of Old Boston and the Old Days." *Springfield Herald* (Springfield, Colorado) May 3, 1918.

[113] Konkel, Sam. "Persons, Stories and Incidents of Old Boston and the Old Days." *Springfield Herald* (Springfield, Colorado) May 10, 1918.

[114] Photo courtesy of Dr. Milligan's great grandson Michael Clark.

[115] Photo courtesy of a shoebox in my mother's basement.

[116] The *Leader-Democrat* (Richfield, Kansas) · 05 Nov 1887, Sat · Page 1

[117] Photo courtesy of a shoebox in my mother's basement.

[118] The Syracuse Journal (Syracuse, Kansas) · 18 Nov 1887, Fri · Page 3

[119] The *Taloga Star* (Taloga, Kansas) · 02 Nov 1888, Fri · Page 3

[120] Capansky Saloon & Billiards Ad, *Boston Banner* (Boston, Colorado), March 8, 1888

[121] Railroad Survey *Boston Banner* (Boston, Colorado), March 8, 1888

[122] Albert W. Thompson, "Old Cow-Outfits of the Cimarron," *The Cattleman,* March, 1928.

[123] *Las Animas Leader* (Las Animas Leader) July 7, 1882.

[124] Austin, J. R. "The Old Towns." *A History of Early Baca County,* 1936

[125] "PIONEER RANCHER," *Baca County Republican,* (Springfield Colorado) Friday June 14, 1935.

[126] Albert W. Thompson, "Neighboring With the Panhandle in the 80s," *The Cattleman,* October 1932.

[127] Photo courtesy of the Baca County Museum, Springfield CO.

[128] Albert. W. Thompson, "Ranching fever raged...when Prairie Cattle Co owned all Outdoors" *The Cattleman*, March 1934.

[129] The *Topeka State Journal* (Topeka, Kansas) · Thur, Aug 2, 1888 · Page 3.

[130] *Colorado Transcript* (Golden CO) Wed September 28, 1887 Page 3. Colorado Historic Newspapers Collection. Colorado State Library.

[131] *Aspen Evening Chronicle* (Aspen CO) Thu August 9, 1888 Page 1. Colorado Historic Newspapers Collection. Colorado State Library.

[132] *Pratt County Times* (Pratt, Kansas) · 02 Mar 1888, Fri · Page 1.

[133] *Minneapolis Star Tribune* (Minneapolis Minnesota) 18 June 1887.

[134] *Colorado Transcript* (Golden CO) Wed September 28, 1887 Page 3 Colorado Historic Newspapers Collection. Colorado State Library.

[135] *Coldwater Review* (Coldwater, Kansas) · 12 Aug 1887, Fri · Page 7.

[136] *Aspen Evening Chronicle* (Aspen CO) April 4, 1889 Page 4 Colorado Historic Newspapers Collection. Colorado State Library.

[137] *Wellington Weekly Quid-Nunc* (Wellington, Kansas) 13 May 1887, Fri ·Page 8.

[138] Jennings, Al. *Beating Back.* Curtis Publishing, 1913.

[139] The *Springfield Republican*, (Springfield, Colorado) Tuesday June 1, 1937. Konkel, Sam. "Persons, Stories and Incidents of Old Boston and the Old Days." *Springfield Herald* (Springfield, Colorado) May 17, 1918.

[141] *Aspen Evening Chronicle*, October 5, 1888. Colorado Historic Newspapers Collection. Colorado State Library.

[142] *Tyrone Daily Herald* (Tyrone, Pennsylvania)·Mon, Oct 8, 1888·Page 1.

[143] *Montreal River Miner and Iron County Republican* (Hurley, Wisconsin) · Thu, Oct 11, 1888 · Page 2.

[144] *The Topeka Daily Capital* (Topeka, Kansas) · Sun, Dec 2, 1888 · Page 4

[145] PIONEER RANCHER," *Baca County Republican*, Springfield Colo. Friday June 14, 1935.

[146] The *Billings Gazette* (Billings, Montana) · 11 Oct 1887, Tue · Page 4

[147] Konkel, Sam. "Persons, Stories and Incidents of Old Boston and the Old Days." *Springfield Herald* (Springfield, Colorado) May 24, 1918.

[148] *Clark County Republican* (Ashland, Kansas) · 18 Feb 1887, Fri · Page 4.

[149] *Morton County Democrat* (Frisco, Kansas) · 12 Feb 1887, Sat · Page 5.

[150] *Oakland Tribune* (Oakland, California) · Sat, Sep 8, 1888 · Page 4.

[151] Konkel, Sam. "Persons, Stories and Incidents of Old Boston and the Old Days." *Springfield Herald* May 31, 1918.

[152] Note: Photos are of poor quality and not used

[153] Konkel, Sam. "Persons, Stories and Incidents of Old Boston and the Old Days." *Springfield Herald* (Springfield, Colorado) May 31, 1918.

[154] Photo provided by the Vilas Museum, Vilas Colorado.

[155] *Buena Vista Democrat* (Buena Vista Colorado) 24 Mar. 1887. Colorado Historic Newspapers Collection. Colorado State Library.

[156] *Trinidad Daily Citizen* (Trinidad, Colorado), 25, 1888 December cited in Tay-lor, Morris. "The Town Boom in Las Animas and Baca Counties." Colorado Magazine, 1978, pp. 126–127.

[157] *Trinidad Daily Citizen*, (Trinidad, Colorado) 25, 1888 December cited in Tay-lor, Morris. "The Town Boom in Las Animas and Baca Counties." Colorado Magazine, 1978, pp. 126–127.

[158] Ashland Clipper (Ashland Kansas) October 27, 1887.
[159] The *Trinidad Daily Citizen* (Trinidad, Colorado) ·27 Feb 1888.
[160] *Greensburg New Era* (Greensburg IN) February 2, 1887.
[161] Map of Colorado 1889." University of Alabama, bit.ly/1889seco. [162]Konkel, Sam. "Persons, Stories and Incidents of Old Boston and the Old Days." *Springfield Herald* (Springfield, Colorado) February 1, 1918.
[163] Konkel, Sam. "Persons, Stories and Incidents of Old Boston and the Old Days." *Springfield Herald* (Springfield, Colorado) February 8, 1918.
[164] *Ulysses Tribune* (Ulysses, Kansas) · 18 Apr 1889, Thu · Page 4.
[165] Konkel, Sam. "Persons, Stories and Incidents of Old Boston and the Old Days." Springfield Herald (Springfield, Colorado) February 22, 1918.
[166] NOTE: The final foundations were removed in the 1970's.
[167] Konkel, Sam. "Persons, Stories and Incidents of Old Boston and the Old Days." *Springfield Herald* (Springfield, Colorado) March 1, 1918.
[168] The Sedalia Weekly Bazoo (Sedalia, Missouri)·Tue, Dec 20, 1887·Page 1. [169] *Western Kansas World* (WaKeeney, Kansas) ·Sat, Dec 24, 1887 · Page 6. [170] *Weekly Republican-Traveler* (Arkansas City, Kansas) · Fri, Dec 23, 1887 · Page 2.
[171] Chappell, Virginia. "Wild Gun Battle Started Decline of Boston in Southeast Colorado." Pueblo Star Journal, 25 July 1954, p. 13c.
[172] NOTE: The marshal was Billy the Kid and not Lew or Lou Reeder.
[173]The *Springfield Republican* (Springfield Colorado) Tuesday June 1, 1937. [174] Emil Lepel was the brother of Frank Lepel.
[175] Springfield Herald (Springfield Co) April 19, 1918.
[176] Konkel, Sam. "Persons, Stories and Incidents of Old Boston and the Old Days." *Springfield Herald* (Springfield, Colorado) January 31, 1919.
[177] *Washington Register* (Washington, Kansas) · 19 Apr 1889, Fri · Page 2.
[178] Konkel, Sam. "Persons, Stories and Incidents of Old Boston and the Old Days." *Springfield Herald* (Springfield, Colorado) January 31, 1919.
[179] *The Democratic Principle* (Syracuse, Kansas) · Wed, Dec 14, 1887.
[180] Konkel, Sam. "Persons, Stories and Incidents of Old Boston and the Old Days." *Springfield Herald* (Springfield, Colorado) April 26, 1919.
[181] J.J. Burnett. Restaurant, Bakery, Groceries and Feed, Advertisement *Baca County Journal* (Boston, Colorado) March 14, 1890.
[182] The *Cuba Daylight* (Cuba, Kansas) · 19 Apr 1889, Fri · Page 2
[183] Konkel, Sam. "Persons, Stories and Incidents of Old Boston and the Old Days." *Springfield Herald* (Springfield, Colorado) February 7, 1919.
[184] Konkel, Sam. "Persons, Stories and Incidents of Old Boston and the Old Days." *Springfield Herald* (Springfield, Colorado) February 14, 1919.
[185] Konkel, Sam. "Persons, Stories and Incidents of Old Boston and the Old Days." *Springfield Herald* (Springfield, Colorado) February 14, 1919.
[186] The *St. Joseph Herald* (St. Joseph, Missouri) · Sun, Apr 14, 1889 · Page 8.
[187] The *Kendall Free Press* (Kendall, Kansas) · 27 Apr 1889, Sat · Page 1.
[188] Konkel, Sam. "Persons, Stories and Incidents of Old Boston and the Old Days." *Springfield Herald* (Springfield, Colorado) February 28, 1919.
[189] Konkel, Sam. "Persons, Stories and Incidents of Old Boston and the Old Days." *Springfield Herald* (Springfield, Colorado) March 7, 1919.

[190]Konkel, Sam. "Persons, Stories and Incidents of Old Boston and the Old Days." *Springfield Herald* (Springfield, Colorado) March 14, 1919.

[191] Konkel, Sam. "Persons, Stories and Incidents of Old Boston and the Old Days." *Springfield Herald* (Springfield, Colorado) March 21, 1919.

[192] Konkel, Sam. "Persons, Stories and Incidents of Old Boston and the Old Days." *Springfield Herald* (Springfield, Colorado) March 28, 1919.

[193] Konkel, Sam. "Persons, Stories and Incidents of Old Boston and the Old Days." *Springfield Herald* (Springfield, Colorado) April 4 1919.

[194] Konkel, Sam. "Persons, Stories and Incidents of Old Boston and the Old Days." *Springfield Herald* (Springfield, Colorado) April 11 1919.

[195] Konkel, Sam. "Persons, Stories and Incidents of Old Boston and the Old Days." *Springfield Herald* (Springfield, Colorado) April 18 1919.

[196] *Westola Wave* (Westola, Kansas) · 19 Apr 1889, Fri · Page 4.

[197] The *Western Star* (Coldwater, Kansas) · 27 Apr 1889, Sat · Page 3.

[198] The *Richfield Monitor* (Richfield, Kansas) · 13 Apr 1889, Sat · Page 2.

[199] *Stevens County Sentinel* (Woodsdale, Kansas) · 19 Apr 1889, Fri · Page 1.

[200] *Stevens County Sentinel* (Woodsdale, Kansas) · 12 Apr 1889, Fri · Page 4.

[201] *Chaffee County Republican* August 21 1915. Page 1. Colorado Historic Newspapers Collection. Colorado State Library.

[202] *Svensk- Amerikanska Western* April 20, 1916 Colorado Historic Newspapers Collection. Colorado State Library.

[203] *Fairplay Flume*, October 19, 1917. Page 1. Colorado Historic Newspapers Collection. Colorado State Library.

[204] *Loveland Daily Herald*, Volume 8, Number 831, August 22, 1917. . Colorado Historic Newspapers Collection. Colorado State Library.

[205] *Rolla Herald* (Rolla, Missouri) · Thu, Jun 28, 1888 · Page 3.

[206] Konkel, Sam. "Persons, Stories and Incidents of Old Boston and the Old Days." *Springfield Herald*, April 25, 1919.

[207](NOTE: At some point it was renamed the Baca County Journal).

[208] (NOTE: I have included a clipping in the succeeding text which shows he was actually from Indiana).

[209] (NOTE: I have included a clipping in this section Smith was buried in Missouri in 1888. I don't think he made it to the Grand Round up).

[210] *Springfield Herald* (Springfield, Colorado) May 2, 1919. Page 1.

[211] NOTE: This was likely true in 1936 but not in the present.

[212] Austin, J. R. "The Old Towns." *A History of Early Baca County*, J.R. Austin, 1936.

[213] The *Philadelphia Inquirer* (Philadelphia, Pennsylvania) · Fri, Sep 26, 1890 · Page 2.

[214] *Los Angeles Herald* (Los Angeles, California) · Fri, Sep 26, 1890 · Page 1 .

[215] *Boston World* (Boston, Colorado) · Thurs March 8, 1887 · Page 1.

[216] Konkel, Sam. "Persons, Stories and Incidents of Old Boston and the Old Days." *Springfield Herald* (Springfield, Colorado) June 7, 1918.

[217] Konkel, Sam. "Joy Unconstrained" The *Western World*, (Boston, Colorado) March 8, 1888.

Old Boston Colorado
-1886-
"That Famous ol' Town"

The author (right) and his cousin, Bill Brooks, standing, March 2018, where Boston,
Colorado's town center, the intersection of 9th and Main Street would have been. This is also
the approximate location of the well where the vigilantes began firing on the cow boys
to begin the seige of Boston April 9, 1889. Nothing is left of the town except the
Colorado prairie in the background.

The Author

Kent Brooks has worked in higher education managing Information Technology and Distance Learning departments for colleges in New Mexico, Oklahoma and Wyoming for more than 20 years. Growing up he listened to southeast Colorado stories about broomcorn, the dust bowl and cowboys of the large cattle companies. He is a long time blogger on various technology topics for his own blog KentBrooks.com as well as the local history blog Bacacountyhistory.com which covers topics about Baca County Colorado, the most southeast county in Colorado. He currently works for Casper College in Casper, Wyoming.